BUILD YOUR ARABIC VOCABULARY

1,000 Key Words to Get Beyond the Basics

HAROON SHIRWANI

McGraw Hill

New York   Chicago   San Francisco   Lisbon   London   Madrid   Mexico City
Milan   New Delhi   San Juan   Seoul   Singapore   Sydney   Toronto

2 3 4 5 6 7 8 9 10 11 12 13 14 15 16 17 18   DOC/DOC   0 9 8 7

ISBN-13: 978-0-07-147876-2
ISBN-10:   0-07-147876-0

McGraw-Hill books are available at special quantity discounts to use as premiums and sales promotions, or for use in corporate training programs. For more information, please write to the Director of Special Sales, Professional Publishing, McGraw-Hill, Two Penn Plaza, New York, NY 10121-2298. Or contact your local bookstore.

This book owes its final form to the efforts, talents and patience of Jane Wightwick and Malmoud Gaafar. My deepest gratitude to them both for their hard work on the design, layout, and illustrations and suggestions regarding the content.

   The learning materials were developed while teaching my first group of students at Eton College. Alex D., Julien M., Joe P., Nick McB., Tim C.J., and Will R.—*lastum mujarrad Tulaab!*

Introduction

Words, words, words! To get ahead in a language, it is important to build up a base of essential vocabulary. The aim of this book is to help you do just that and, moreover, to make the process as efficient and interesting as possible.

ABOUT THIS BOOK

Each topic covers an area of everyday life, and contains a list of *core vocabulary*, some *further vocabulary*, and then a series of *exercises*. The core vocabulary is also provided on *flashcards*. In addition, the book contains *language tips* to help you remember certain key points of Arabic grammar and spelling. Finally, there is a section with *examination advice*.

Core vocabulary: the key words that will help you build a foundation in each topic area.

Further vocabulary: this will supplement the core vocabulary and enhance your command of the language.

Exercises: the purpose of the exercises is to bring the vocabulary to life. They will help you progress from recognizing the words to actually using them, seeing how they relate to each other and making them yours. They start with the most basic words and then increase in sophistication. A final freer exercise allows you to express yourself using your new vocabulary.

Flashcards: an invaluable aid to help you memorize the core vocabulary. You can take the words with you wherever you go.

Language tips: these explain small points of grammar and spelling to help you use the words with greater confidence.

Examination advice: this section contains advice on exam preparation. There is also a list of questions and instructions (rubrics) which frequently appear in public examinations.

You'll find suggestions and tips on using this book on pages 6–7.

Contents

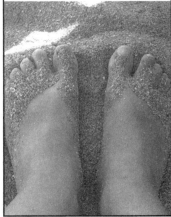

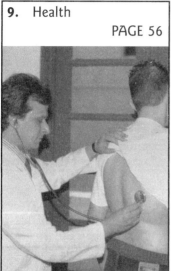
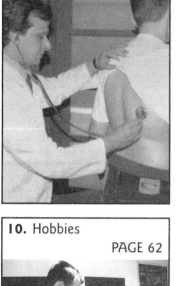

640 Arabic–English tear-out vocabulary flashcards

How to use this book

AS A STUDENT

If you are studying on your own, here is one way of working through the book:

1   Start with the core vocabulary, using the flashcards to help you. (Advice on using the flashcards is given below.) Take your time in getting to know these essential words, perhaps over the course of a few days, until you feel comfortable with them.
2   Then take a look at the further vocabulary and phrases. Just try and familiarize yourself with these. There is no need to memorize them.
3   Now it is time to try the exercises. As much as possible, make use of the words you can remember, without looking them up. When you have been through the exercises once, refer back to the lists to see which words you need to review.
4   The final exercises are more open-ended than the others and give you space for personal expression. Feel free to use the words that interest you the most. If you have access to a teacher or a friend who knows Arabic, perhaps you can ask them to look over your work and tell you what they think.

If you are attending a course, you can use this book to reinforce and enrich your learning: the word lists and flashcards will give you vocabulary to supplement what you have learned in class; the language tips will highlight and explain the most important grammatical points; the basic exercises will allow you to test your knowledge; and the writing exercises will improve your composition skills.

AS A TEACHER

If you are a teacher, this book is a key classroom tool. Each topic serves as either reinforcement or a point of departure for the study of different aspects of everyday life. The flashcards, exercises and tips can be used to back up and complement the material covered in class, and can also be the basis for classroom activities.

TIPS FOR LEARNING VOCABULARY

1   Relax! You will take in a lot more if you are at ease and having fun.
2   Say the words out loud. The vocabulary does not just exist on paper – it is meant to be spoken. Repeat each word over and over so that you feel comfortable saying it. The transliteration is provided to help you with this.

3 Carry the flashcards around with you. Whenever you have a spare moment, take them out and go through a few.

4 Use the flashcards as labels, especially for everyday items. Stick them onto the items they refer to so that you associate them with their Arabic name.

5 Use the flashcards to store the words in your long-term memory. Here is how:
- Take five envelopes and label them I to 5.
- Place the flashcards for a topic in envelope I.
- Go through the cards and place the words you know into envelope 2 and keep the rest in envelope I.
- The next week, go through them again. If you still know a word in envelope 2, move it along to envelope 3. If you know a word from envelope I, move it along to envelope 2. If you do not know a word, put it back in envelope I.
- Each week, do the same, moving the cards to the next envelope if you know the word, or back to envelope I if you do not. Keep going until all the words are in envelope 5.

6 Play a memory game. Lay the flashcards for a topic out on a table, with the Arabic face up. Choose a card and say the meaning of the word out loud. Then turn the card over to check. If you got the meaning right, you can take the card away. If not, put it back and try another card. Once you can do this, turn all of the cards over and try the same thing, but this time from English into Arabic.

7 If you are having difficulty learning a particular word, stick its flashcard onto something you use a lot, such as a refrigerator. Each time you want to use that item, you have to say the word and its meaning before you can go any further!

8 Work with someone else. Test each other on the vocabulary and go through the exercises together. A shared activity can be more enjoyable and motivating.

HOW THE VOCABULARY IS PRESENTED

I All words in the vocabulary lists are transliterated to help with pronunciation.

2 Arabic plurals are either *sound* (ending in ون/ين for sound masculine plural, ات for sound feminine plural) or *broken* (various forms). It is worth learning the plural with the singular. Plurals are given in brackets for most nouns, e.g. بَيت (بُيوت).

3 You can assume adjectives use the sound plurals unless otherwise shown.

4 Each verb is given in the past tense and then the present tense, always in the third person masculine ('he') form, e.g. سكَنَ، يَسكُنْ.

TOPIC 1
Greetings and basics

💡 CORE VOCABULARY

welcome	marHaban	مَرحَبًا
hello, hi	ahlan	أهلاً
hello and welcome	ahlan wa sahlan	أهلاً وَسَهلاً
welcome to you *(reply)*	ahlan bik (*f* biki)	أهلاً بِك (بِكِ)
peace be on you	as-salaamu ᶜalaykum	السَّلامُ عَلَيكُم
and on you be peace *(reply)*	wa ᶜalaykum as-salaam	وعَلَيكُم السَّلام
pleased to meet you	tasharrafnaa	تَشَرَّفنا
good morning	SabaaH al-khayr	صَباح الخَير
good morning *(reply)*	SabaaH an-nuur	صَباح النور
good evening	masaa' al-khayr	مَساء الخَير
good evening *(reply)*	masaa' an-nuur	مَساء النور
please	min faDlak (*f* min faDlik)	مِن فَضلَك (مِن فَضلِك)
thanks (for)	shukran (ᶜala)	شُكرًا (على)
excuse me, you're welcome	ᶜafwan	عَفوًا
sorry	aasif	آسِف
what? *(followed by noun)*	maa	ما؟
what? *(followed by verb)*	maadha	ماذا؟
who?	man	مَن؟
where?	ayna	أينَ؟
when?	mataa	مَتى؟
how?	kayfa	كَيفَ؟

why?	limaadha	لِماذا؟
God willing	in shaa' allaah	إن شاء اللّه
happy to have met you	furSa saᶜiida	فُرصَة سَعيدة
goodbye	maᶜ as-salaama	مَع السَّلامة
I	ana	أنا
you (m, f)	anta, anti	أنتَ ، أنتِ
you (mpl, fpl)	antum, antunna	أنتُم ، أنتُنَّ
we	naHnu	نَحنُ
he	huwa	هُوَ
she	hiya	هِيَ
they (m, f)	hum, hunna	هُم ، هُنَّ
in	fii	في
on	ᶜala	عَلى
from	min	مِن
to, for	li	لِ
with	maᶜa	مَعَ
above	fawqa	فَوقَ
below	taHta	تَحتَ
beside	bijaanib	بِجانِب

FURTHER VOCABULARY

good night	tiSbaH (f tiSbaHi) ᶜala khayr	تصبح (تصبحي) عَلى خَير
good night (reply)	wa anta (f anti) min ahluh	وأنتَ من أهله
help!	an-najda	النَّجدة!
don't mention it	laa shukr ᶜala waajib	لا شُكر على واجِب
no trouble	laa ba's	لا بَأس
it's not a problem	laysat mushkila	لَيسَت مُشكلة
until we meet (again)	ilal-liqaa'	إلى اللقاء
see you tomorrow/soon	araaka (f araaki) ghadan/qariiban	أراك غَدًا\ قَريبًا
Dear...	ᶜaziizi (f ᶜaziizati)	عَزيزي... (عَزيزتي...)

Regards	maʿa taHiyyaati	مَعَ تَحيّاتي
many happy returns *(for all special occasions)*	kull ʿaam wa antum bi-khayr/ kull sana wa antum Tayyibuun	كُلُّ عام وَأنتُم بخَير كُلُّ سَنة وَأنتُم طَيّبُون
happy holiday/happy Eid	ʿiid saʿiid	عيد سَعيد
happy birthday	(ʿiid) miilaad sa3iid	(عيد) ميلاد سَعيد
happy Ramadan	ramaDaan kariim	رَمَضان كَريم
blessed holiday	ʿiid mubaarak	عيد مُبارك
Christmas	ʿiid al-miilaad	عيدالميلاد
Easter	ʿiid al-fiSH	عيدالفصح
with best wishes	maʿa aTyab at-taHiyyaat	مَعَ أطيَب التَحيّات
thus has God willed *(always used approvingly)*	ma shaa' allaah	ما شاء الله
God give you strength	allaah yuTiik (f yuTiiki) al-ʿaafiya	الله يُعطيك (يُعطيك) العافية
God bless you	allaah yubaarik fiik (f fiiki)	الله يُبارك فيك (فيكِ)
opposite	muqaabil	مُقابِل
between	bayna	بَينَ
inside (the...)	daakhil (il...)	داخِل (الـ...)
outside (the...)	khaarij (il...)	خارِج (الـ...)
toward	ila	إلى
around	Hawla	حَولَ

 # USEFUL PHRASES

My name is...	أنا اِسمي...
What's your name?	ما اسمك؟
Where are you from?	أنتَ مِن أينَ؟
I'm from the United States/Britain.	أنا مِن أمريكا/بريطانيا.
How are you?	كَيفَ الحال؟
I'm fine, thanks be to God.	بخَير الحَمد لله.

EXERCISES

I. Look at the pictures and decide what the people are saying to each other, choosing from the expressions in the box below, as in the example.

٥ تصبحي على خير	١ وأنت من أهله
٦ صباح النور	٢ صباح الخير
٧ مساء الخير	٣ شكرًا
٨ عفوًا	٤ مساء النور

2. Each of these people is referring to a particular person or group. Match the pronouns to the pictures.

أنا

أنتَ

هي

نحن

هنّ

3. Where's the cat? Use an appropriate preposition (in, on, etc.) to say where the cat (القطّة al-qiTTa) is in relation to the car (السّيارة as-sayyaara):

١ القطّة _____ السّيارة.

٢ القطّة _____ السّيارة.

٣ القطّة _____ السّيارة.

٤ القطّة _____ السّيارة.

4. You are sending a card to your friend, Ahmad, on his birthday. Write a brief message, using phrases from the list. Some of the words are given as clues.

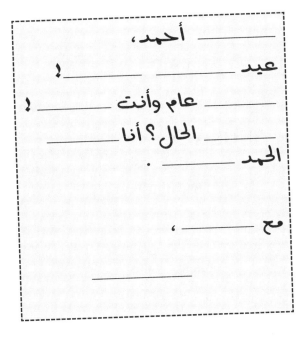

_____ أحمد،

عيد _____ _____ !

_____ عام وأنت _____ !

_____ الحال؟ أنا _____

الحمد _____ .

مع _____ ،

_____

 REMEMBER

الـ... al- ("the") has these features:

- it is written joined to the following noun: قطّة qiTTa (a cat), القطّة al-qiTTa (the cat);

- the pronunciation varies depending on the opening sound of the following noun: القطّة al-qiTTa (the cat), but السيّارة as-sayyaara (the car);

- it elides with the previous word if this ends with a vowel: في السيّارة fis-sayyaara (in the car); نحنُ المدرّسون naHnu l-mudarrisuun (we're the teachers).

TOPIC 2

House and home

CORE VOCABULARY

to live, reside	sakana, yaskun	سكَنَ، يَسكُن
house	bayt (buyuut)	بَيت (بُيوت)
home, dwelling	manzil (manaazil)	منزِل (مَنازِل)
apartment	shaqqa (shuqaq)	شَقّة (شُقَق)
villa	fillaa (fillaat)	فيلا (فيلات)
apartment block	ʿimaara (ʿimaaraat)	عمارة (عمارات)
district, area	minTaqa (manaaTiq)	مِنطَقة (مَناطِق)
old	qadiim	قَديم
modern	Hadiith	حَديث
quiet, calm	haadi'	هادِئ
crowded	muzdaHim	مُزدحِم
comfortable	muriiH	مُريح
to consist (of)	takawwana, yatakawwan (min)	تَكَوّنَ، يَتَكَوّن (من)
floor *(level)*	Taabiq (Tawaabiq)/ duur (adwaar)	طابِق (طَوابِق)/ دور (أدوار)
room	ghurfa (ghuraf)	غُرفة (غُرَف)
bedroom	ghurfat an-nawm	غُرفة النَّوم
sitting room	ghurfat al-juluus	غُرفة الجُلوس
living room	ghurfat al-maʿiisha/aS-Saaluun	غُرفة المَعيشة/الصالون
dining room	as-sufra	السُفرة
office, study, desk	maktab (makaatib)	مَكتَب (مَكاتِب)

kitchen	maTbakh (maTaabikh)	مَطبَخ (مَطابِخ)
bathroom	Hammaam (Hammaamaat)	حَمّام (حَمّامات)
garden, yard, park	Hadiiqa (Hadaa'iq)	حَديقة (حَدائق)
street	shaaric (shawaaric)	شارع (شَوارِع)
to rent	ista'jara, yasta'jir	استَأجَرَ، يَستَأجِر
rent	iijaar	ايجار
furnished	mafruush	مَفروش
carpet	sijaada (sijaad)	سِجادة (سِجاد)
curtain	sitaara (sataa'ir)	سِتارة (سَتائر)
sofa	kanaba (kanab, kanabaat)	كَنَبة (كَنَب، كَنَبات)
bed	sariir (asirra)	سَرير (أسِرّة)
oven	furn (afraan)	فُرن (أفران)
refrigerator	thallaaja (thallaajaat)	ثَلّاجة (ثَلّاجات)
table	maa'ida (mawaa'id)	مائدة (مَوائد)
chair	kursii (karaasii)	كُرسي (كَراسي)
door	baab (abwaab)	باب (أبواب)
window	shubbaak (shabaabiik)	شُبّاك (شَبابيك)
bell	jaras (ajraas)	جَرَس (أجراس)
air-conditioning	takyiif [al-hawaa']	تَكييف [الهَواء]
elevator	miScad (maSaacid)	مِصعَد (مَصاعِد)

FURTHER VOCABULARY

reception room	ghurfat al-istiqbaal	غرفة الاستِقبال
hall/reception area	Saala	صالة
stairs, ladder	sullam	سُلَّم
garage	garaaj (garaajaat)	جَراج (جَراجات)
swimming pool	Hammaam as-sibaaHa	حمّام السباحة
furniture	athaath	أثاث
to move (to)	intaqala, yantaqil (ilaa)	انتَقَلَ، يَنتَقِل (إلى)
place	makaan (amaakin)	مَكان (أماكِن)

agency	wikaala (wikaalaat)	وِكالة (وِكالات)
for sale	lil-bayᶜ	للبيع
parking space	mawqif sayyaara (mawaaqif sayyaaraat)	مَوقِف سَيّارة (مَواقِف سيّارات)
it is situated in (m/f)	yaqaᶜ fii/taqaᶜ fii	يَقَع في/تَقَع في

USEFUL PHRASES

We have a house with three bathrooms.	عندنا بيت بثلاثة حمّامات.
The ground floor (U.S. "first floor") consists of the kitchen, dining room and living room.	يتكوّن الطابق الأرضي من المطبخ، السفرة وغرفة المعيشة.
I live in an apartment on the first floor (U.S. "second floor") of a large apartment block.	أسكُن في شقّة في الدور الأوّل من عمارة كبيرة.
My house is situated in the district of Zamalik.	يقع منزلي في منطقة الزمالك.
I'd like to rent a furnished apartment.	أريد أن أستأجر شقّة مفروشة.
My room is small but it's comfortable.	غرفتي صغيرة ولكنّها مريحة.

REMEMBER

Arabic is a cursive, or "joined up" script. Words are not generally written as separated letters. The main exception to this is crosswords and word squares. The Arabic solutions run right to left or top to bottom, and the letters are written in their separate, complete form. For example, the word قديم (old) would be written like this:

across ق د ي م   down ق
                          د
                          ي
                          م

If a word is written with a shadda (ّ), this letter will be repeated twice in the word squares in this book, for example (reading left to right): شقّة = ش ق ق ة.

EXERCISES

1. Complete the crossword using the Arabic equivalents of the words in the list. (Read the tip on page 16 before you start.)

Across		Down	
office	١	place	١
air-conditioning	٤	house	٢
home/dwelling	٦	rent (noun)	٣
floor	٧	oven	٥

2. Label the pictures with the appropriate adjective in the box below.

١ هادئ

٢ قديم

٣ جديد

٤ مزدحم

3. Translate the sentences below. Remember that if the noun is feminine, the adjective needs ـة / ة.

a   The house is large.   _____

b   The villa is old.   _____

c   The elevator is crowded.   _____

d   The apartment is new and furnished. _____

e   The room is comfortable.   _____

4. Label the rooms in the house, using the words in the box.

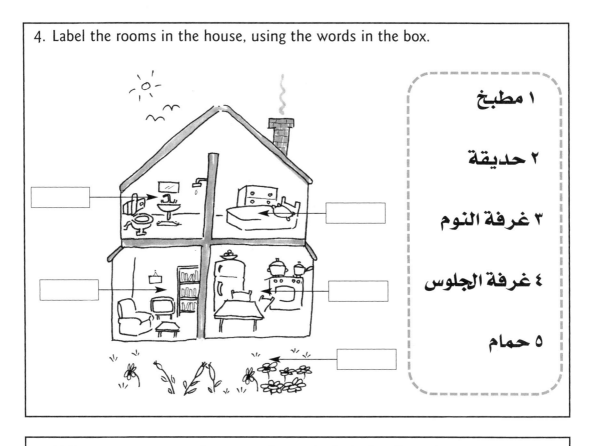

١ مطبخ

٢ حديقة

٣ غرفة النوم

٤ غرفة الجلوس

٥ حمام

5. Write 3–4 sentences about your home. Include details such as:

- whether it's a house or an apartment (how many floors?)

- a short description (quiet? comfortable? large?, etc.)

- one or two details about the individual rooms

_____

_____

_____

_____

_____

TOPIC 3

Family and friends

CORE VOCABULARY

family *(immediate)*	usra (usar)	أُسرة (أُسَر)
family *(extended)*	ᶜaa'ila (ᶜaa'ilaat)	عائلة (عائلات)
relative	qariib (aqaarib)	قَريب (أقارب)
father	ab (aabaa')	أب (آباء)
mother	umm (ummahaat)	أُمّ (أُمَّهات)
parents	waalidaan/waalidayn	والدان/والدَين
brother	akh (ikhwa)	أخ (إخوة)
sister	ukht (akhawaat)	أُخت (أَخَوات)
son	ibn (abnaa')	ابن (أبناء)
daughter	ibna (banaat)	ابنة (بَنات)
wife	zawja (zawjaat)	زَوجة (زوجات)
husband	zawj (azwaaj)	زَوج (أزواج)
boy	walad (awlaad)	وَلَد (أولاد)
girl	bint (banaat)	بِنت (بَنات)
uncle *(paternal)*	ᶜamm (aᶜmaam)	عَمّ (أعمام)
uncle *(maternal)*	khaal (akhwaal)	خال (أخوال)
aunt *(paternal)*	ᶜamma (ᶜammaat)	عَمّة (عمّات)
aunt *(maternal)*	khaala (khaalaat)	خالة (خالات)
grandfather	jadd (ajdaad)	جَدّ (أجداد)
grandmother	jadda (jaddaat)	جَدّة (جَدّات)
grandson	Hafiid (aHfaad)	حَفيد (أحفاد)

granddaughter	Hafiida (Hafiidaat)	حَفيدة (حَفيدات)
nephew	ibn al-akh/al-ukht	ابن الأخ/الأخت
niece	bint al-akh/al-ukht	بِنت الأخ/الأخت
bride	ᶜaruus (ᶜaraa'is)	عَروس (عَرائس)
bridegroom	ᶜariis (ᶜursaan)	عَريس (عُرسان)
married	mutazawwij	مُتَزوِّج
marriage	zawaaj	زواج
divorced	muTallaq	مُطَلَّق
divorce	Talaaq	طَلاق
single (m)	ᶜazab (ᶜuzzaab)	أعزَب (عُزّاب)
single (f)	ᶜazbaa' (ᶜaazibaat)	عَزباء (عازِبات)
child	Tifl (aTfaal)	طِفل (أطفال)
man	rajul (rijaal)	رَجُل (رِجال)
woman	imraa'a (nisaa')	امرأة (نِساء)
youth	shaabb (shabaab, shubbaan)	شابّ (شَباب، شُبّان)
friend	Sadiiq (aSdiqaa')	صَديق (أصدِقاء)
to be born	wulida, yuulad	وُلِدَ، يُولَد
to die	maata, yamuut	ماتَ، يَموت
to get married	tazawwaja, yatazawwaj	تَزوّجَ، يَتَزوّج

FURTHER VOCABULARY

members of the family	afraad al-ᶜaa'ila	أفراد العائلة
fiancée	khaTiiba (khaTiibaat)	خَطيبة (خَطيبات)
fiancé	khaTiib (khuTabaa')	خَطيب (خُطَباء)
separated	munfaSil	مُنفَصِل
twin	taw'am (tawaa'im)	تَوأم (تَوائم)
girl, young woman	fataa (fatayaat)	فَتاة (فَتَيات)
boy, young man	Sabiyy, Sibyaan	صَبيّ (صِبيان)
friend, owner	SaaHib (aSHaab)	صاحب (أصحاب)
adult	raashid (raashiduun/iin)	راشِد (راشِدون/ين)

mother-in-law	Hamaa (Hamawaat)	حماة (حموات)
father-in-law	Ham (aHmaa')	حَم (أحماء)
cousin *(uncle's son, uncle's daughter, etc.)*	ibn ᶜamm, bint khaal, etc.	ابن عمّ، بنت خال …
adolescent	muraahiq (muraahiquun/iin)	مُراهِق (مُراهِقون/ين)
orphan	yatiim (aytaam)	يَتيم (أيتام)
widower	armal (araamil)	أرمَل (أرامِل)
widow	armala (araamil)	أرمَلة (أرامِل)
ancestors	ajdaad	أجداد
to name	samma, yusammii	سمّى، يُسمّي
to be introduced (to), to first meet	taᶜarrafa, yataᶜarraf (ᶜala)	تَعَرَّفَ، يَتَعَرَّف (على)
to bring up	rabba, yurabbii	ربّى، يُربّي
to be brought up	tarabba, yatarabba	تَرَبّى، يَتَرَبّى
to adopt	tabanna, yatabanna	تَبَنّى، يَتَبَنّى

 # USEFUL PHRASES

Who's this *(m/f)*?	مَن هذا/هذِه؟
This is my friend, Maha.	هذِه صَديقتي مَها.
This is my brother, Mark.	هذا أخي مارك.
Pleased to meet you.	تَشَرَّفنا. / فُرصة سَعيدة.
I have a friend whose name is Hassan.	لي/عِندي صاحِب اِسمُه حَسَن.
I was born in ... *(place)*.	وُلِدتُ في …
My mother was born in the year	وُلِدَت أمي في سَنة ….
My grandfather died last year.	مات جَدّي السَنة الماضية.
I first met my friend Sara at school.	تَعَرَّفتُ عَلى صَديقتي سارة في المَدرَسة.

---

1. How many of the words from the list can you find?

أ	ف	ء	ث	ا	س	ن
س	ع	د	ا	ل	و	أ
ر	ن	م	ك	ط	ج	أ
ة	س	و	ر	ع	ح	ع
ة	ض	ص	ث	غ	ه	ز
ى	ق	ي	د	ص	س	ب
أ	ر	ب	ب	ا	ش	ل
ر	ؤ	س	ن	ي	ب	ص
م	ب	ز	ا	ع	ا	ه
ل	ش	ئ	ت	ز	ظ	ر

family

girls

boys

widower

bride

friend

youth

single (*m*)

boy, young man

---

2. Fill in the gaps in the family tree.

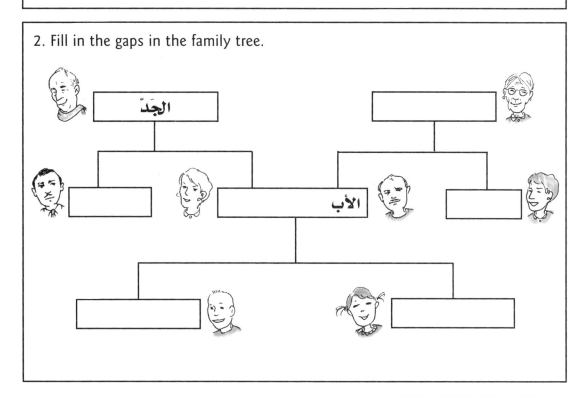

الجَدّ

الأب

3. Fill the boxes with synonyms (words with the same meaning) or near-synonyms.

```
┌─────────────┐
│             │
└────────┐    │
         │  ┌──────────┐        ┌──────────┐
         │  │  صديق     │        │  صديقة    │
         │  └──────────┘        └────┐─────┘
                                     │  ┌──────────────┐
                                     │  │              │
                                     │  └──────────────┘

        ┌──────────────┐         ┌──────────┐
        │              │         │  أَسرة    │
        └───┐          │         └───┬──────┘
┌──────────┐│ ┌──────────┐           │  ┌──────────────┐
│  وَلَد      ├┼─┤          │           │  │              │
└──────────┘│ └──────────┘           │  └──────────────┘
            │ ┌──────────────┐  ┌──────────────┐
            │ │              │  │              │
┌──────────┐  └──────────────┘  └──────────────┘
│          │
└──────────┘
```

4. Complete the following sentences.

١ مات زَوج صَديقتي. هي ــــــــــــ . ـ

٢ أُختي سَتَتَزَوَّج في سَبتَمبِر. تَعَرَّفَت عَلى ــــــــــــ ــــــــــــها في الجامعة.

٣ أُم زوجتي هي ــــــــــــ ـي .

٤ عندي أربعة ــــــــــــ : ثلاث بنات ووَلَد.

5. Write 4–5 sentences about your family and friends. Include details such as:

- how many brothers and sisters or children you have (+ names)
- where and when you and other family members were born
- the name(s) of friend(s) and where you met them

_____

_____

_____

_____

_____

_____

_____

_____

_____

_____

 REMEMBER

When أب *ab* (father), أخ *akh* (brother) and حم *ham* (father-in-law) are put in front of another noun or a possessive ending ("his," "her," etc.), they usually become أبو *abuu*, أخو *akhuu* and حمو *hamuu*: أبو سامي *abuu saami* (Sami's father), أخوها *akhuuhaa* (her brother), حمو دينا *hamuu diinaa* (Dina's father-in-law).

The main exception is for "my": أبي *abi* (my father), أخي *akhi* (my brother).

TOPIC 4
Character and feelings

💡 CORE VOCABULARY

personality, character	shakhSiyya	شَخصيّة (شَخصيّات)
manners, morals	akhlaaq	أخلاق
feelings	shuʿuur	شُعُور
not, non-, un- (+ noun/adjective)	ghayr	غَير
nice	laTiif (luTafaa')	لَطيف (لُطَفاء)
pleased	saʿiid (suʿadaa')	سَعيد (سُعَداء)
happy	masruur	مَسرور
sad	Haziin (Hazaanaa)	حَزين (حَزانى)
truthful	Saadiq	صادق
sorry	aasif	آسِف
funny	muDHik	مُضحك
distressing	mu'sif	مُؤسِف
exciting	muthiir	مُثير
amazing	ʿajiib	عَجيب
different	mukhtalif	مُختَلف
similar	mushaabih	مُشابه
strange	ghariib	غريب
normal, usual	ʿaadii	عادي
boring	mumill	مُملّ
strong	qawii (aqwiyaa')	قوي (أقوياء)
weak	Daʿiif (Duʿfaa')	ضَعيف (ضُعَفاء)

angry (m/f)	ghaDbaan/ghaDbaa (ghiDaab)	غَضبان / غَضبى (غِضاب)
shy	khajuul	خَجول
generous	kariim (kiraam)	كَريم (كِرام)
miserly	bakhiil (bukhalaa')	بَخيل (بُخلاء)
intelligent	dhakii (adhkiyaa')	ذَكي (أذكياء)
stupid	ghabii (aghbiyaa')	غَبي (أغبياء)
lazy	kasuul	كَسول
energetic	nashiiT (nishaaT)	نَشيط (نِشاط)
well-behaved	mu'addab	مُؤَدّب
afraid (of)	khaa'if (min)	خائِف (مِن)
joyful	farHaan	فَرحان
very	jiddan	جِدّاً
a little	qaliilan	قَليلاً
completely	tamaaman	تَمامًا
to believe, to think	iᶜtaqada, yaᶜtaqid	اعتَقَدَ ، يَعتَقِد
to think, to reflect	fakkara, yufakkir	فكّرَ ، يُفَكِّر
to like	aHabba, yuHibb	أحَبَّ ، يُحِبّ
to dislike, to hate	kariha, yakrah	كَرِهَ ، يَكرَه
to feel	shaᶜara, yashᶜur bi-	شَعَرَ ، يَشعُر بِ

FURTHER VOCABULARY

mood, temperament	mizaaj (amzija)	مِزاج (أمزِجة)
loyal	wafii (awfiyaa')	وَفي (أوفياء)
sincere	mukhliS	مُخلِص
patient	Sabuur	صَبور
serious	jaadd	جادّ
hard-working	mujtahid	مُجتَهِد
famous	mash-huur	مَشهور
noisy	Daajj	ضاجّ
quiet	haadi'	هادِئ

rudeness, lack of manners	qillat al-adab	قلّة الأدَب
amazement, surprise	dahsha	دَهشة
shame	ᶜayb	عَيب
disappointment	khaybat al-amal	خَيبة الأمَل
loneliness	wiHda	وحدة
fear	khawf	خَوف
excitement	ithaara	إثارة
surprising	mud-hish	مُدهِش
horrible	faZiiᶜ	فَظيع
pleasant	Zariif (Zurafaa')	ظَريف (ظُرَفاء)
selfish	anaanii	أناني
reasonable	maᶜquul	مَعقول
nervous	ᶜaSabii	عَصَبي
honorable	shariif (shurafaa')	شَريف (شُرفاء)
wise	Hakiim (Hukamaa')	حَكيم (حُكَماء)
brave	shujaaᶜ (shujᶜaan)	شُجاع (شُجعان)
to smile	ibtasama, yabtasim	إبتَسَمَ ، يَبتَسِم
to laugh	DaHika, yaD-Hak	ضَحِكَ ، يَضحَك
to cry	bakaa, yabkii	بَكى ، يَبكي
to lie	kadhaba, yakdhib	كَذَبَ ، يَكذِب

USEFUL PHRASES

My father is in a good mood today.	والِدي حَسَن المِزاج اليوم.
Yesterday he was in a bad mood.	أمس كان سيّء المِزاج.
I feel shy/lonely.	أشعُر بالخَجل / بالوحدة.
I was disappointed.	خاب أمَلي.
He can't stand the sight of me ("hates me to blindness").	يكرهني للعَمى.
She was in floods of tears ("crying with heat").	كانَت تَبكي بحَرارة.
Loneliness is better than bad company. (proverb)	الوحدة خَير مِن جليس السوء.

TOPIC 4
EXERCISES

1. Find words from the main vocabulary list to describe the people in the pictures.

_____ ٣   _____ ٢   _____ ١

_____ ٦   _____ ٥   _____ ٤

---

2. Write down the opposites of the adjectives below.

_____   ١ سعيد

_____   ٢ نشيط

_____   ٣ ضاجّ

_____   ٤ ذكي

_____   ٥ بخيل

3. From the vocabulary list, put the adjectives (صِفات) into these categories:

- very positive (إيجابيّة جِدًّا)
- positive (إيجابيّة)
- negative (سَلبيّة)
- very negative (سَلبيّة جِدًّا)

سَلبيّة جِدًّا	سَلبيّة	إيجابيّة	إيجابيّة جِدًّا

 REMEMBER

أَنّ (anna) means *that*, in the sense of "I think *that*…," "it is possible *that*…" or "among his good points is *that* he's…". أَنّ takes the attached pronoun:

أَنّ + هو = أَنّه (that he/it) annahu

أَنّ + هي = أَنّها (that she/it) annahaa

أعتقد أنّه شخص غريب جدًا *I think that he's a very strange person*

4. Here is a short paragraph in which someone describes the personality of a cousin, Leila:

اِسمها ليلى وهي بنت عمّي. تسكُن في نيو يورك. هي هادئة جدًا. من صفاتها
الايجابية أنّها ذكيّة وكريمة وصادقة. من صفاتها السلبية أنّها كسولة.
لا أعتقد أنها مُجتهدة في المدرسة.

Now write a similar paragraph about someone you know, or a famous person.
Use the following phrases to help you:

● his/her name is...	اِسمه/اِسمها...
● he/she is from...	هو/هي من...
● he/she lives in...	يَسكُن/تَسكُن في...
● among his/her positive characteristics is that he/she...	من صفاته/صفاتها الايجابية أنّه/أنّها...
● among his/her negative characteristics is that he/she...	من صفاته/صفاتها السلبية أنّه/أنّها...

_____

_____

_____

_____

_____

Shopping

🧠 CORE VOCABULARY

store	maHall (maHallaat)/ dukkaan (dakaakiin)	مَحَلّ (مَحَلّات)/ دُكّان (دَكاكين)
open	maftuuH	مَفتوح
closed	maqfuul/mughlaq	مَقفول/مُغلَق
market	suuq (aswaaq)	سوق (أسواق)
shopping mall	markaz (maraakiz) at-tasawwuq	مَركَز (مَراكِز) التَّسَوُّق
price	siʿr (asʿaar)/ thaman (athmann)	سِعر (أسعار)/ ثَمَن (أثمان)
cash (money)	naqd (nuquud)	نَقد (نُقود)
money, wealth	maal (amwaal)	مال (أموال)
inexpensive	rakhiiS	رَخيص
expensive (indefinite/definite)	ghaalin/al-ghaalii	غالٍ/الغالي
sale, offer	ʿarD (ʿuruuD)	عَرض (عُروض)
seller	baaʼiʿ (baaʿa)	بائِع (باعة)
merchant	taajir (tujjaar)	تاجِر (تُجّار)
bakery	makhbaz (makhaabiz)	مَخبَز (مَخابِز)
butcher	jazzaar (jazzaaruun/-iin)	جَزّار (جَزّارون/ين)
fishmonger	sammaak (sammaakuun/-iin)	سَمّاك (سمّاكون/ين)
grocery store	baqqaal (baqqaaluun/-iin)	بَقّال (بقّالون/ين)
perfume/spice seller	ʿaTTaar (ʿaTTaaruun/-iin)	عَطّار (عطّارون/ين)
tailor	khayyaaT (khayyaaTuun/-iin)	خَيّاط (خيّاطون/ين)
jeweller	Saaʼigh (Suyyaagh)	صائغ (صُيّاغ)

wallet	miHfaZa (maHaafiZ)	مِحفَظة (مَحافظ)
bag, case	Haqiiba (Haqaa'ib)	حَقيبة (حَقائب)
sack, bag	kiis (akyaas)	كيس (أكياس)
copper	nuHaas	نُحاس
silver	fiDDa	فِضّة
gold	dhahab	ذَهَب
leather	jild	جلد
wood	khashab	خَشَب
free	majjaanii	مَجاني
gift	hadiya (hadaaya)	هَدية (هَدايا)
few, a little	qaliil	قَليل
many, much	kathiir	كَثير
account, check (total payable)	Hisaab (Hisaabaat)	حساب (حسابات)
receipt	iiSaal (iiSaalaat)	إيصال (إيصالات)
reduction, discount	takhfiiD (takhfiiDaat)	تَخفيض (تَخفيضات)
to pay	dafaᶜa, yadfaᶜ	دَفَع، يَدفَع
to buy	ishtara, yashtarii	اشترى، يَشتَري
to give	aᶜTaa, yuᶜTii	أعطى، يُعطي
to cost	kallafa, yukallif	كَلَّفَ، يُكَلّف
it is found, located (m/f)	yuujad/tuujad	يُوجَد / تُوجَد

FURTHER VOCABULARY

section	qism (aqsaam)	قسم (أقسام)
bottle	zujaaja (zujaajaat)	زُجاجة (زجاجات)
pack, tin	ᶜulba (ᶜulab)	عُلبة (عُلَب)
box	Sunduuq (Sanaadiiq)	صُندوق (صَناديق)
handbag	Haqiibat yad (Haqaa'ib yad)	حَقيبة يَد (حَقائب يَد)
handmade	shughl yad	شُغل يَد
ivory	ᶜaaj	عاج
check (bank)	shiik (shiikaat)	شيك (شيكات)

travelers' checks	shiikaat siyaaHiyya	شيكات سياحية
credit card	biTaaqat (biTaaqaat) i'timaan	بِطاقة (بِطاقات) ائتِمان
guarantee	Damaan (Damaanaat)	ضَمان (ضَمانات)
currency	ᶜumla (ᶜumlaat)	عُملة (عُملات)
exchange (office)	(maktab) Siraafa	(مَكتَب) صِرافة
cashier	Sarraaf (Sarraafuun/-iin)	صَرّاف (صَرّافون/ين)
exchange rate	siᶜr as-Sarf	سِعر الصَرف
the change	al-baaqii	الباقي
tax	Dariiba (Daraa'ib)	ضَريبة (ضَرائب)
trader, store	matjar (mataajir)	مَتجَر (مَتاجِر)
traditional	taqliidii	تَقليدي
natural	Tabiiᶜii	طَبيعي
artificial	muSTanaᶜ	مُصطَنَع
fake	muzayyaf	مُزَيَّف
to open	fataHa, yaftaH	فَتَحَ، يَفتَح
to close	aghlaqa, yughliq/qafala, yaqfil	أغلَقَ، يُغلِق/قَفَلَ، يَقفِل
to choose	ikhtaara, yakhtaar	اختارَ، يَختار
to exchange (an item)	istabdala, yastabdil	استَبدَلَ، يَستَبدِل
to change (money)	Sarrafa, yuSarrif	صَرّفَ، يُصَرّف
to agree (e.g. on a deal)	ittafaqa, yattafiq	اتَّفَقَ، يَتَّفِق

USEFUL PHRASES

May I help you? ("any service?")	أيّ خِدمة؟
How much is this?	بِكَم هذا؟
I want a suitable gift for my mother.	أريد هَدية مُناسِبة لأمي.
Is this the final price?	هَل هذا آخَر سِعر؟
Do you arrange shipping?	هل تُرَتِّبون الشَحن؟
When does the store shut?	مَتى يُغلَق المحلّ؟

EXERCISES

1. Choose a word from the list below to describe each of the pictures

زجاجة	خيّاط
مغلق	مفتوح
حقيبة	سمّاك
رخيص	غالٍ

2. Match the store signs with the activities:

A Have your shirt mended

B Change travelers' checks

C Browse for souvenirs

D Buy a packet of sugar

E Find a bargain

F Try out some local perfumes

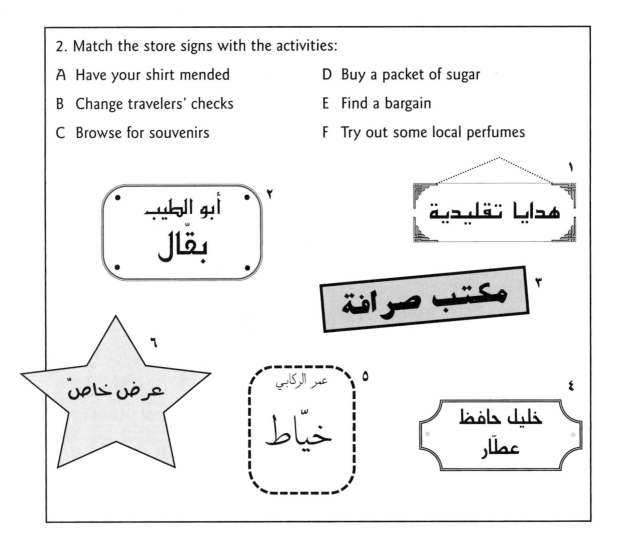

١ هدايا تقليدية

٢ أبو الطيب بقّال

٣ مكتب صرافة

٤ خليل حافظا عطّار

٥ عمر الركابي خيّاط

٦ عرض خاصّ

3. Circle the odd-one-out in each set of words.

نحاس	فضّة	عُملة	١ ذهب
متجر	شيك	محلّ	٢ دكّان
طبيعي	حساب	تقليدي	٣ مزيّف
قسم	محفظة	كيس	٤ حقيبة

4. Make six sentences about a shopping trip, using the grid below to help you construct the sentences. The first column _on the right_ gives you expressions to say _when_ you went; the next column gives verbs of movement; the next says _where_ you went; the remaining columns show how to say _why_ you went.

items	shopping verbs	intention	places, people	verbs of movement	expressions of time
بَعْضَ الـ... (some...)	أشتَري/ نَشتري (buy)	لِـ... (to)	السّوق (the market)	ذَهَبْتُ إلى (I went to)	في الصَّباح (in the morning)
هَدايا (gifts)	أختار/ نَختار (choose)	حتّى (in order to)	الدُّكان (the shop)	ذَهَبْنا إلى (we went to)	بعد الظُّهر (in the afternoon)
مَلابِس (clothes)	استَبْدِل/ نَستبدِل (exchange)		البنك (the bank)	مَشيتُ إلى (I walked to)	في المَساء (in the evening)
شيكات (checks)	أصرِّف/ نصرِّف (change)		البَقّال (the grocer)	مَشينا إلى (we walked to)	أوَّلاً (firstly)
etc. (see vocabulary)			etc. (see vocabulary)		ثُمَّ (then)
					بعد ذلك (after that)

example: في الصَّباح ذهبـنا إلى السوق لِنشتري بعض الهدايا
وبعد ذلك مشينا إلى البنك حتّى نصرّف الشيكات.

 REMEMBER

- In Arabic, we literally say: "I went to the market so that I (may) buy some clothes" (ذهبتُ إلى السوق لأشتري ملابس). So, after لِـ... _li_ and حَتّى _Hatta_, you need to use the present tense in the same person as the subject.

- If you want to talk about the material something is made from, add يّ -_ii_ to make the noun for the material into an adjective:

  leather (noun ⇨ adjective)   جلد + يّ = جلديّ

  leather bag (feminine, so add ة):   حقيبة جلديّة

TOPIC 6

Clothes and colors

CORE VOCABULARY

clothing	malaabis	ملابس
garments	thiyaab	ثياب
uniform (outfit)	ziyy (azyaa')	زِيّ (أزياء)
underwear	malaabis daakhiliyya	مَلابِس داخِليّة
size, measurement	qiyaas/miqaas	قياس/مقاس
comfortable	muriiH	مُريح
shirt	qamiiS (qumSaan)	قَميص (قُمصان)
pants	sirwaal (saraawiil), banTaluun (banTaluunaat)	سِروال (سَراويل)، بَنطَلون (بَنطَلونات)
shoe	Hidhaa' (aHdhiya)	حِذاء (أحذِية)
sandal	Sandal (Sanaadil)	صَندَل (صَنادِل)
jacket	sutra (sutar), jaakiitta (jaakiittaat)	سُترة (سُتَر)، جاكيتّة (جاكيتّات)
suit	badla (bidal)	بَدلة (بِدَل)
dress	fustaan (fasaatiin)	فُستان (فَساتين)
skirt	tannuura (tannuuraat), jiiba (jiibaat)	تنّورة (تنّورات)، جيبة (جيبات)
blouse	bluuza (bluuzaat)	بلوزة (بلوزات)
coat	miʿTaf (maʿaaTif)	مِعطَف (مَعاطِف)
glove	quffaaz (quffaazaat)	قُفّاز (قُفّازات)
sock	jawrab (jawaarib)	جَورَب (جَوارِب)
hat	qubbaʿa (qubbaʿaat)	قُبّعة (قُبّعات)

belt	Hizaam (aHzima)	حِزام (أحزِمة)
headscarf (Islamic)	Hijaab (aHjiba)	حِجاب (أحجِبة)
cloth/textile	qumaash (aqmisha)	قُماش (أقمِشة)
wool	Suuf	صُوف
cotton	quTn	قُطن
silk	Hariir	حَرير
black (m/f)	aswad/sawdaa'	أسوَد/سوداء
red (m/f)	aHmar/Hamraa'	أحمَر/حَمراء
yellow (m/f)	aSfar/Safraa'	أصفَر/صَفراء
blue (m/f)	azraq/zarqaa'	أزرَق/زَرقاء
white (m/f)	abyaD/bayDaa'	أبيَض/بَيضاء
green (m/f)	akhDar/khaDraa'	أخضَر//خَضراء
brown	bunnii	بُنّي
orange	burtuqaalii	بُرتُقالي
violet	banafsajii	بَنَفسَجي
pink	wardii	وَردي
purple	urjuwaanii	أُرجُواني
light (color)	faatiH	فاتِح
dark, deep (color)	ghaamiq	غامِق
to wear	labisa, yalbas	لَبِسَ، يَلبَس
to take off	khalaʿa, yakhlaʿ	خَلَعَ، يَخلَع

FURTHER VOCABULARY

fashion	moDa	موضة
sleeve	kumm (akmaam)	كُمّ (أكمام)
collar	yaaqa (yaaqaat)	ياقة (ياقات)
pocket	jayb (juyuub)	جَيب (جُيوب)
label	ʿalaama (ʿalaamaat)	عَلامة (عَلامات)
jeans	jiinz	جينز
sweater	kanza	كنزة

raincoat	miˁTaf (maˁaaTif) maTarii	مِعطَف (مَعاطِف) مَطَري
tie	rabTat (ribaaT) al-ˁunuq	رَبطة (رباط) العُنُق
scarf	wushaaH (wushuH)	وُشاح (وُشُح)
buckle	mishbak (mashaabik)	مِشبَك (مَشابِك)
sole	naˁl (niˁaal)	نَعل (نعال)
waistcoat	Sudayriyya (Sudayriyyaat)	صُديرِيّة (صُديرِيّات)
ring	khaatim (khawaatim)	خاتِم (خواتِم)
earring	qirT (aqraaT)	قرط (أقراط)
necklace	qilaada (qalaa'id)	قلادة (قلائد)
to put on	irtadaa, yartadii	ارتدى، يرتدي
to iron	kawaa, yakwii	كوى، يَكوي
to repair	aSlaHa, yuSliH	أصلحَ، يُصلِح

 USEFUL PHRASES

These clothes suit you	هذه الملابس لائقة عَليك.
What's your size?	كَم مِقاسك؟
Is this silk/cotton/wool?	هَل هذا حَرير/قُطن/صوف؟
I'd prefer the color to be darker/lighter.	أفضل أن يكون اللون أغمَق/أفتَح
Eat what you like, and wear what other people would like. *(proverb)*	كُل ما يُعجِبك والبَس ما يُعجِب الناس.

 REMEMBER

Non-human plurals are grammatically feminine singular in Arabic. What does this mean? It means that when talking about clothing, groceries and other items, then all the verbs, pronouns, and adjectives you use with them must be in the *feminine singular*. So how do you say "These clothes are comfortable. I like them a lot"?

Wrong	✗ هؤُلاء الملابس مُريحون. أحبّهُم كثيراً.
Right	✔ هذه الملابس مُريحة. أحبّها كثيراً.

(Notice in the vocabulary list that the feminine for some colors is irregular.)

TOPIC 6
EXERCISES

1. Find words in the vocabulary list to describe the pictures below.

٥ _____

٢ _____

٧ _____

٦ _____

٣ _____

١ _____

٨ _____

٤ _____

2. Circle the odd-one-out in each set of words.

ثياب	ملابس	قلادة	١ زيّ
كنزة	بلوزة	قميص	٢ بنطلون
مقاس	صوف	حرير	٣ قطن
وردي	حذاء	أزرق	٤ أسود

3. Maryam is a very tidy person. She has a shelf for each type of clothing.

Shelf 1: upper body clothing (blouses, sweaters, etc.)
Shelf 2: lower body clothing (pants, skirts, etc.)
Shelf 3: jewelry
Shelf 4: accessories (hats, scarves, etc.)
Shelf 5: footwear

Maryam is at work, and her little sister Salma has just been through her closet and taken all the items out to try them on, but can't remember where everything goes. Can you help Salma put everything back in the right place before Maryam gets back?

Write the shelf number next to the item in the box below, as in the example.

جورب ☐	قفّاز ☐	بلوزة ☐	بنطلون ☐ 2
جينز ☐	تنّورة ☐	خاتم ☐	قلادة ☐
صندل ☐	حذاء ☐	حزام ☐	سترة ☐
قرط ☐	كنزة ☐	قبّعة ☐	وشاح ☐

4. You are about to go clothes shopping for you and your family. Make eight sentences about what they like to wear, and what you plan to buy for them. Use the table below to help you (starting with the *right-hand* column).

for whom	description (adjectives)	clothing	to buy/ to wear	want/like
لِأُمّي (for my mother)	كَبير/ كبيرة (large)	ملابس (clothes)	أن أشتري (to buy – "I")	أُريد (I want)
لأخي (for my brother)	صغير/ صغيرة (small)	قُمصانًا (shirts)	أن ألبس (to wear – "I")	أُحبّ (I like)
لِابني (for my son)	قَصير/ قصيرة (short)	أحذية (shoes)	أن يَشتري (to buy – "he")	يُريد (he wants)
لِبنتي (for my daughter)	جَميل/ جميلة (beautiful)	حزامًا (a belt)	أن يلبس (to wear – "he")	يُحبّ (he likes)
etc. (see Topic 3 vocabulary)	أخضَر/ خضراء (green)	بلوزة (a blouse)	أن تَشتري (to buy – "she")	تُريد (she wants)
	etc. (see vocabulary)	etc. (see vocabulary)	أن تلبس (to wear – "she")	تُحبّ (she likes)

example:

أريد أن أشتري قمصانًا بيضاء لأخي.
أخي يحبّ أن يلبس قمصانًا كبيرة.

 REMEMBER

You might be wondering why قُمصـانًا and حزامًا in the table above have acquired an *alif* and are vowelled with ̋ (-*an*). If a word without ة or ـال *al-* is the object of a sentence (so something is happening to it), it usually has this additional ending. E.g.:

I want to buy a belt for my daughter.   أُريد أن أشتري حزامًا لِبنتي.

You don't often hear this ending in everyday speech because it is generally a feature of more formal spoken or written Arabic.

Food and drink

💡 CORE VOCABULARY

food	Taᶜaam/akl	طَعام/أكل
menu, list	qaa'ima (qawaa'im)	قائمة (قَوائم)
dish, course	Tabaq (aTbaaq)	طَبَق (أطباق)
meal	wajba (wajbaat)	وَجبة (وَجبات)
sugar	sukkar	سُكَّر
butter	zubda	زُبدة
salt	milH	مِلح
pepper	filfil	فِلفِل
bread	khubz	خُبز
rice	aruzz	أرُزّ
oil	zayt	زَيت
cheese	jubna	جُبنة
eggs	bayD	بَيض
meat	laHm	لَحم
lamb, mutton	(laHm) Da'nii	(لحم) ضَأني
beef	(laHm) baqarii	(لحم) بَقَريّ
pork	laHm al-khinziir	لحم الخِنزير
chicken	dajaaj	دَجاج
fish	samak	سَمَك
vegetables	khuDrawaat	خُضرَوات
fruit	fawaakih	فَواكه

salad	salaTa	سَلَطة
onions	baSal	بَصَل
potatoes	baTaaTaa/baTaaTis	بَطاطا/ بَطاطِس
carrots	jazar	جَزَر
olives	zaytuun	زَيتُون
grapes	ᶜinab	عِنَب
apples	tuffaaH	تُفّاح
oranges	burtuqaal	بُرتُقال
lemons	laymuun	لَيمون
bananas	mawz	مَوز
milk	Haliib	حَليب
juice	ᶜaSiir	عَصير
water	maa'	ماء
coffee	qahwa	قَهوة
tea	shaay	شاي
alcohol	kuHuul	كُحُول
dessert, sweet	Halwaa	حَلوى
to eat	akala, ya'kul	أكَلَ، يأكُل
to drink	shariba, yashrab	شَرِبَ، يشرَب

FURTHER VOCABULARY

can, tin, box	ᶜulba (ᶜulab)	عُلبة (عُلَب)
canned food	muᶜallabaat	مُعَلّبات
plate	SaHn (SuHuun)	صَحن (صُحون)
cooking pot	qidr (quduur)	قِدر (قُدور)
vinegar	khall	خَلّ
sausages	sujuq	سُجُق
chocolate	shuukuulaata	شُوكُولاتة
mushrooms	fiTr	فِطر
cauliflower	qarnabiiT	قَرنَبيط

dates	balaH/tamr	بَلَح/تَمر
figs	tiin	تين
cherries	karaz	كَرَز
raisins	zabiib	زَبيب
pineapple	anaanaas	أناناس
strawberry	faraawla	فَراولة
green salad	salaTa khaDraa	سَلَطة خَضراء
vegetarian	nabaatii	نَباتي
fried	maqlii	مَقلي
barbecued, grilled	mashwii	مَشوي
boiled	masluuq	مَسلوق
drink	mashruub (mashruubaat)	مَشروب (مَشروبات)
mineral water	maa' maᶜdanii	ماء مَعدَني
cola	kola	كولا
wine	nabiidh	نَبيذ
beer	biira	بيرة
to eat (a meal)	tanaawala, yatanaawaal (wajba)	تَناوَلَ، يَتناوَل (وجبة)
to taste	dhaaqa, yadhuuq	ذاقَ، يذوق
to have breakfast	faTara, yafTur	فَطَرَ، يَفطُر
to have lunch	taghaddaa, yataghaddaa	تَغَدّى، يَتَغَدّى
to have dinner	taᶜshshaa, yataᶜshshaa	تَعَشّى، يَتَعَشّى

 ## USEFUL PHRASES

"Eat well!", "Bon appétit!"	هَنيئًا!/بالهَنا!
"Health and well-being!"	صحّة وعافية!
I'd like a kilo of apples please.	أريد كيلو تفّاح من فضلك.
Tea with milk, please.	شاي بِالحليب، مِن فضلك.
I drink coffee without sugar.	أشرَب القَهوة بِدون سُكّر.

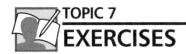

TOPIC 7
EXERCISES

1. Choose a word from the list below to describe each of the pictures.

عصير	سمك
قدر	دجاج
خبز	قهوة
شاي	جزر

2. You have just returned from the market (السوق), and need to unload the shopping into the refrigerator (الثلاجة). Put each item from the box below in the right section.

فواكه fruit

المشروبات drinks

الخضروات vegetables

حليب	بصل	برتقال	فطر
عنب	تفّاح	عصير تفاح	ماء
عصير برتقال	كولا	كرز	قرنبيط
فراولة	جزر	زيتون	موز

3. Circle the odd-one-out in each set of words.

زيت	دجاج	ملح	١ فلفل
ماء	عصير	زبدة	٢ قهوة
علبة	قدر	طبق	٣ قائمة
حلوى	بصل	زيتون	٤ جزر

4. Describe your eating habits. You should say what time you have your meals and what you normally eat. Use the tables below to help you (starting with the *right-hand* columns).

adverb	time (minute)	time (hour)	meal	how often?
تمامًا (exactly)	والنصف (half after)	الساعة الواحدة (at 1 o'clock)	أَفطُر (I have breakfast)	عادةً (usually)
تَقريبًا (approximately)	والرُبع (quarter after)	الساعة الثانية (at 2 o'clock)	أَتَغَدَّى (I have lunch)	أحيانًا (sometimes)
	إلا رُبعًا (quarter to)	الساعة الثالثة (at 3 o'clock), etc.	أَتَعَشَّى (I have dinner)	دائمًا (always)

condiment	with/without	food/drinks	eat/drink	meal
سُكَّر (sugar)	بِـ... (with)	سلطة (salad)	آكُل (I eat)	للفَطور (for breakfast)
خَلّ (vinegar)	بِدون (without)	قهوة (coffee)	أشرَب (I drink)	للغَداء (for lunch)
etc. (see vocabulary)		etc. (see vocabulary)	أُفضِّل (I prefer)	للعَشاء (for dinner)

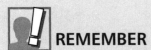 REMEMBER

Here is how you tell the time in Arabic:

English	Formal Arabic	Colloquial Arabic
(at) four o'clock	الساعة الرابعة "the fourth hour"	الساعة أربعة "hour four"
(at) quarter after five	الساعة الخامسة والرُبع "the fifth hour and the quarter"	الساعة خمسة والرُبع "hour five and the quarter"

The body

CORE VOCABULARY

body	jism (ajsaam)	جِسم (أجسام)
skeleton	haykal (hayaakil) ᶜaZmii	هَيكل (هياكِل) عَظمِيّ
head	ra's (ru'uus)	رَأس (رُؤوس)
face	wajh (wujuuh)	وَجه (وُجوه)
eye (f)	ᶜayn (ᶜuyuun)	عَين (عُيون)
ear (f)	udhun (aadhaan)	أُذُن (آذان)
nose	anf (unuuf)	أنف (أُنوف)
mouth	fam (afwaah)	فَم (أفواه)
tongue	lisaan (alsina)	لِسان (ألسِنة)
neck	raqaba (riqaab)	رَقَبة (رِقاب)
belly, stomach	baTn (butuun)	بَطن (بُطون)
arm (f)	dhiraaᶜ (adhruᶜ)	ذِراع (أذرُع)
leg (f)	rijl (arjul)/ saaq (siiqaan)	رِجل (أرجُل)/ ساق (سيقان)
foot (f)	qadam (aqdaam)	قَدَم (أقدام)
knee	rukba (rukab)	رُكبة (رُكَب)
hand (f)	yad (ayaadin)	يَد (أياد)
elbow	kuuᶜ (akwaaᶜ)/ mirfaq (maraafiq)	كوع (أكواع)/ مِرفَق (مَرافِق)
wrist	rusgh (arsaagh)	رُسغ (أرساغ)
shoulder	kitf (aktaaf)	كِتف (أكتاف)
tooth	sinn (asnaan)	سِنّ (أسنان)

finger	iSba⁣ᶜ (aSaabi⁣ᶜ)	إصبَع (أصابِع)
toe	iSba⁣ᶜ ar-rijl (aSaabi⁣ᶜ ar-rijl)	إصبَع الرِّجل (أصابِع الرِّجل)
thumb	ibhaam	إبهام
chest	Sadr (Suduur)	صَدر (صُدُور)
back	Zahr (Zuhuur)	ظَهر (ظُهُور)
heart	qalb (quluub)	قَلب (قُلوب)
hair	sha⁣ᶜr	شَعر
brain	mukhkh	مُخّ
blood	dam	دَم
lung	ri'a (ri'aat)	رِئة (رِئات)
lip	shafa (shifaah)	شَفة (شِفاه)
bone	⁣ᶜaZm (⁣ᶜiZaam)	عَظم (عِظام)
skin	jild (juluud)	جِلد (جُلود)
to see	ra'a/yara	رأى \ يرى
to hear	sami⁣ᶜa/yasma⁣ᶜ	سَمِعَ \ يَسمَع
to smell	shamma/yashumm	شَمَّ \ يَشُمّ
to taste	dhaaqa/yadhuuq	ذاقَ \ يَذُوق
to move (something)	Harraka/yuHarrik	حَرَّكَ \ يُحَرِّك
to move (yourself)	taHarraka/yataHarrak	تَحَرَّك \ يَتَحَرَّك
to touch	lamisa/yalmas	لَمِسَ \ يَلمَس

REMEMBER

Parts of the body that occur in pairs are often feminine, for example:

a large foot   *qadam kabiira* قدم كبيرة

the ear hears   *al-udhun tasma⁣ᶜ* الأُذُن تَسمَع

When referring to these pairs together, you need to use the dual (*-aan*) in the feminine, for example:

long legs   *rijlaan Tawiilataan* رِجلان طويلتان

FURTHER VOCABULARY

muscle	ʿaDala (ʿaDalaat)	عَضَلة (عَضَلات)
fat	dihn (duhuun)	دِهن (دُهون)
kidney	kulya (kulan)	كُلية (كُلى)
throat	Hanjara (Hanaajir)	حَنجَرة (حَناجِر)
chin	dhiqn (dhuquun)	ذَقن (ذُقون)
cheek	khadd (khuduud)	خَدّ (خُدود)
eyebrow	Haajib (Hawaajib)	حاجِب (حَواجِب)
eyelash	rimsh (rumuush)	رِمش (رُموش)
moustache	shaarib (shawaarib)	شارِب (شَوارِب)
beard	liHya (liHan)	لِحية (لِحىً)

 USEFUL PHRASES

I have a pain in my leg.	عِندي أَلَم في رِجلي.
Her hair is long and black.	شَعرها أَسود وطَويل.
I'll be happy to do it! ("on my eyes and head")	عَلى عَيني ورَأسي!
He is light-hearted. ("his blood is light")	دَمُه خَفيف.
She is unpleasant. ("her blood is heavy")	دَمُها ثَقيل.
He uses abusive language. ("his tongue is long")	لِسانه طَويل.

1. How many of the words from the list can you find?

ش	و	م	ك	ة	ى	ظ
ي	ج	ن	ط	ب	لا	ه
س	ه	ن	ط	و	ر	ر
أ	ع	ب	ص	إ	ؤ	ل
ن	ب	ت	م	ز	ء	ب
ف	ل	ا	ن	ظ	م	ف
ع	م	ا	ه	ب	إ	ل
غ	ق	ث	ص	ض	ئ	ر
ع	ا	ر	ذ	ه	ع	غ

back

mouth

thumb

finger

arm

stomach

nose

face

2. Match up each sense with the relevant part of the body.

(with my ____)	(I ____ ...)
بِيَدي	أذوق ...
بِأُذُني	أرى ...
بِأَنفي	أسمع ...
بِعَيني	ألمس ...
بِلِساني	أشمّ ...

3. Label the parts of the body, using the vocabulary list to help you.

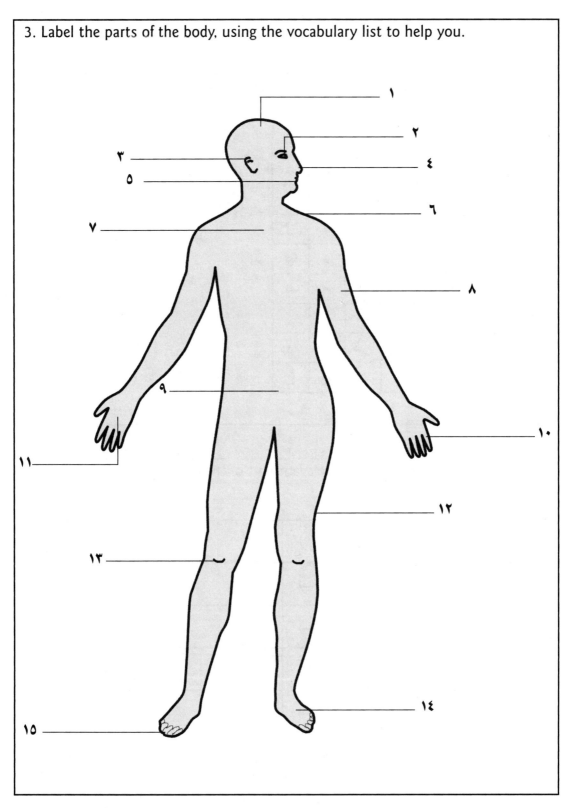

١

٢

٣

٤

٥

٦

٧

٨

٩

١٠

١١

١٢

١٣

١٤

١٥

4. Describe yourself or someone you know, based on the table below.

adjectives *feminine dual*	adjectives *feminine/non- human plural*	adjectives *masculine singular*	parts of the body	have	negation *"do not (have)"*
جميلتان *(beautiful)*	جميلة *(beautiful)*	جميل *(beautiful)*	وجه *(face)*	عندي / لي *(I have)*	لَيسَ *(masculine)*
صغيرتان *(small)*	صغيرة *(small)*	صغير *(small)*	شعر *(hair)*	عندكَ / لكَ *(you m. have)*	لَيسَت *(feminine)*
طويلتان *(long)*	طويلة *(long)*	طويل *(long)*	أنف *(nose)*	عندك / لكِ *(you f. have)*	
صَفرايان *(yellow/fair)*	صَفراء *(yellow/fair)*	أصفر *(yellow/fair)*	عينان *(eyes)*	عنده / لَه *(he has)*	
سَودايان *(black)*	سَوداء *(black)*	أسود *(black)*	رموش *(eyelashes)*	عندهـا / لَها *(he has)*	
etc. (see vocabulary)	etc. (see vocabulary)	etc. (see vocabulary)	etc. (see vocabulary)		

 REMEMBER

In the table we have given two ways of saying "have": عند *ᶜind* and لـ... *li/la...* .

• In colloquial Arabic, عند is more common.

• In formal Arabic, both are found. However, لـ... usually refers to something that belongs to you. For this reason, it is not generally used with symptoms or illnesses:

I have a car. *(that belongs to me)*   لي سيّارة.

I have a pain in my leg. *(at this moment in time)*   عِندي ألَم في رِجلي.

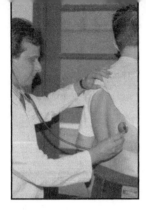

Health

CORE VOCABULARY

health	siHHa	صحّة
healthy	bi-siHHa jayyida	بصحّة جيّدة
illness	maraD (amraaD)	مَرَض (أمراض)
sick, patient (noun)	mariiD (marDa)	مَريض (مَرْضى)
cold	bard	بَرد
congested (nose)	mazkuum	مَزكوم
afflicted with	muSaab bi	مُصاب بـ
fever	Humma	حُمّى
diarrhoea	is-haal	إسهال
cough	suᶜaal	سُعال
pulse	nabaD	نَبَض
headache	Sudaaᶜ	صُداع
injury	iSaaba (iSaabaat)	إصابة (إصابات)
wound	jurH (jiraaH)	جُرح (جراح)
pain	alam (aalaam)	أَلَم (آلام)
painful	mu'lim	مُؤلِم
medicine	dawaa' (adwiya)	دَواء (أدوية)
pill	Habba (Hubuub)	حَبّة (حُبوب)
tablet	qurS (aqraaS)	قُرص (أقراص)
thermometer	miqyaas al-Haraara	مِقياس الحَرارة
accident	Haadith (Hawaadith)	حادِث (حَوادث)

hospital	mustashfa (mustashfayaat)	مُستشفى (مُتسَشفيات)
doctor	Tabiib (aTibbaa')	طَبيب (أطبّاء)
nurse	mumarriDa (mumarriDaat)	مُمرّضة (مُمرّضات)
ambulance	sayyarat is'aaf	سَيّارة إسعاف
operation, surgery	jiraaHa (jiraaHaat)	جِراحة (جِراحات)
doctor's office	'iyaada ('iyaadaat)	عِيادة (عيادات)
cure	shifaa' (ashfiya)	شِفاء (أشفية)
treatment	'ilaaj ('ilaajaat)	عِلاج (علاجات)
habit	'aada ('aadaat)	عادة (عادات)
addicted (to)	mudmin ('ala)	مُدمِن (على)
smoking	tadkhiin	تَدخين
diet	rajiim	رجيم
to suffer (from)	'aanaa, yu'aanii (min)	عانَى، يُعاني (مِن)
to take (medicine, etc.)	tanaawal, yatanaawal	تَناوَل، يَتَناوَل
to fall	waqa', yaqa'	وَقَعَ، يَقَع
to break	kasara, yaksar	كَسَر، يَكسِر
to cough	sa'ala, yas'ul	سَعَلَ، يَسعُل
to swallow	bala'a, yabla'	بَلَعَ، يَبلَع
to smoke	dakhkhana, yudakhkhin	دَخّنَ، يُدَخّن

FURTHER VOCABULARY

first aid	is'aafaat awwaliyya	إسعافات أوّليّة
wheelchair	kursii naqqaal	كُرسي نَقّال
protection	wiqaaya	وِقاية
cancer	saraTaan	سَرَطان
allergy	Hassaasiyya	حَسّاسية
diabetes	maraD as-sukkarii	مَرَض السُكّري
virus	fayruus (fayruusaat)	فيروس (فيروسات)
influenza	influwenza	إنفلوَنزا
chicken pox	judarii l-maa'	جُدَري الماء

measles	HaSba	حَصبة
mumps	nukaaf	نُكاف
mental illness	maraD ᶜaqlii	مَرَض عَقلي
stress	at-tawattur	التَوَتُّر
bruise	kadma (kadmaat)	كَدمة (كدمات)
blister	qarHa (qiraH)	قَرحة (قِرَح)
swelling	waram (awraam)	وَرَم (أورام)
scar	nadba (andaab)	نَدبة (أنداب)
sunstroke	Darbat shams	ضَربة شَمس
blood pressure	DaghT ad-dam	ضَغط الدَم
pregnant	Haamil	حامِل
to sneeze	ᶜaTaSa, yaᶜTas	عطَسَ، يَعطِس
to gargle	tagharghara, yatagharghar	تَغَرغَرَ، يَتَغَرغَر
to give up *(e.g. smoking)*	aqlaᶜa, yuqliᶜ ᶜan	أقلَعَ، يُقلِع عَن

 USEFUL PHRASES

I've had *("I feel")* a headache since the morning.	أشعُر بصداع مُنذُ الصَّباح.
What do you have for diarrhoea?	ماذا عِندكُم لِلإسهال؟
Call an ambulance!	أطلُبوا الإسعاف!
The injury is serious.	الإصابة جَسيمة.
She broke her leg.	كَسَرَت رِجلها.
Is the doctor coming now?	هل سَيَأتي الطَبيب الآن؟
I'm pregnant in my fifth month.	أنا حامِل في الشَهر الخامِس.

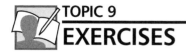

EXERCISES

1. How many of the words from the list below can you find in the word search? Read the tip on page 16 before you start.

ص	ا	أ	ب	ع	غ	ف	إ
ح	ج	ل	ص	د	ا	ع	س
ح	م	م	ى	ع	ع	غ	ه
ة	د	ح	ج	ج	ح	خ	ا
ذ	م	د	ن	س	ع	ا	ل
د	ن	ذ	ب	ب	ل	ل	ب
ذ	د	د	ض	ع	ا	د	ة
ز	ل	ا	م	ب	ج	ل	ب
ت	د	خ	ي	ن	ا	ل	ر
ظ	ة	ئ	ء	ؤ	ئ	ء	د

health	smoking	fever
addicted	treatment	headache
pain	habit	diarrhoea
cold	cough	pulse

2. Find as many words as you can that link to the headings below:

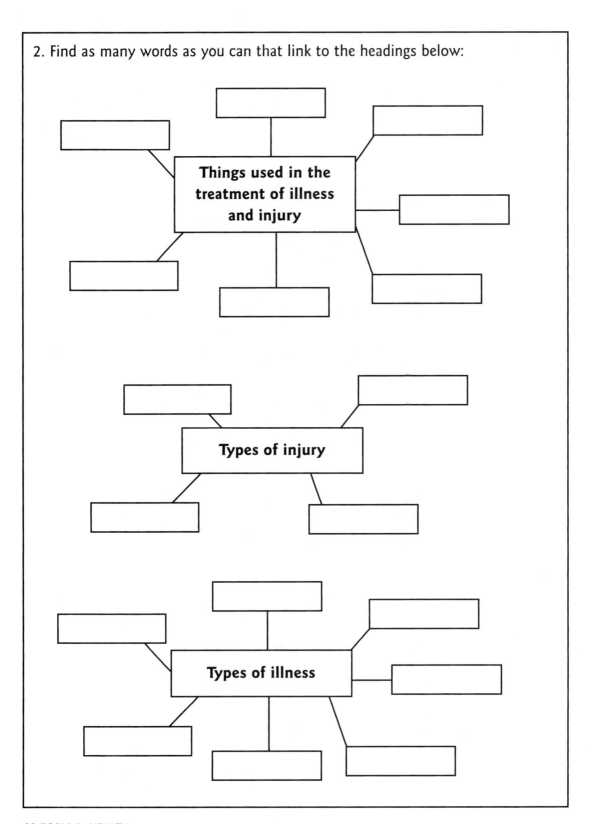

Things used in the treatment of illness and injury

Types of injury

Types of illness

3. Complete the following sentences, using the verbs in the box below.

١ أنا مُدمِن على التَدخين. عادةً ‫_____‬ أربعين سيجارة كلّ يوم.

٢ مُنذُ يَوم الحادِث وهو ‫_____‬ التوتُّر في السيّارة.

٣ بعد العشاء ‫_____‬ فاطمة بألَم في بَطنها.

٤ ما لَكِ تعطسين و ‫_____‬ طول الوقت؟ هل عندك برد؟

شَعَرَت	تَسعُلين	أدَخِّن	يُعاني مِن

REMEMBER

Many Arabic verbs need to be followed by a particular preposition (مِن *min*, بـ *bi-*, عن *ʿan*, etc.). This may or may not reflect the situation in the English. For example:

He suffers from diabetes.	يعاني من مرض السكّري.
I feel lonely. (*"I feel loneliness."*)	أشعُر بالوحدة.
She gave up smoking.	أقلَعَت عن التَدخين.

Hobbies

🧠 CORE VOCABULARY

hobby	hiwaaya (hiwaayaat)	هِواية (هِوايات)
spare time	waqt al-faraagh	وَقت الفَراغ
sport	riyaaDa	رِياضة
sporty, sportsman	riyaaDii	رِياضيّ
game	luᶜba (alᶜaab)	لُعبة (ألعاب)
player	laaᶜib (laaᶜibuun/-iin)	لاعِب (لاعِبون/ين)
team	fariiq (firaq)	فَريق (فِرَق)
training, practice	tadriib (tadriibaat)	تدريب (تدريبات)
soccer	kurat al-qadam	كُرة القَدَم
basketball	kurat as-salla	كُرة السَلّة
volleyball	al-kura aT-Taai'ra	الكُرة الطائِرة
running, jogging	jarii/ᶜadw	جري/عَدو
skiing	tazalluj	تَزَلُّج
swimming	sibaaHa	سِباحة
dancing	raqS	رَقص
music	muusiiqaa	مُوسيقى
singing	ghinaa'	غِناء
group, band	firqa (firaq)	فِرقة (فِرَق)
song	ughniya (aghaanin)	أُغنية (أَغانٍ)
singer	mughannin (mughanniyuun/-iin)	مُغَنٍّ (مُغَنّيون/ين)
musical instrument	aala (aalaat) muusiqiyya	آلة (آلات) موسيقية

flute	fluut	فلوت
violin	kamaan	كمان
guitar	giitaar	جيتار
piano	biyaanuu	بيانو
horn, trumpet	buuq (abwaaq)	بوق (أبواق)
drum	Tabla (Tubuul)	طَبلة (طُبول)
reading	qiraa'a/muTaala3a	قراءة/مُطالَعة
watching movies	mushaahadat al-aflaam	مُشاهَدة الأفلام
play (theater)	masraHiyya (masraHiyyaat)	مَسرَحيّة (مَسرَحيّات)
drawing	rasm	رَسم
photography	taSwiir	تَصوير
hunting	Sayd	صَيد
fishing	Sayd al-samak	صَيد السَمَك
chess	shaTranj	شَطرَنج
backgammon	Taawila (az-zahr)	طاوِلة (الزهر)
board game	lu3ba lawHiyya	لَعبة لوحية
to play (a sport)	la3iba, yal3ab	لَعبَ ، يَلعَب
to play (an instrument)	3azafa, ya3zif 3alaa	عَزَفَ ، يعزِف على
to be interested in	ihtamma, yahtamm bi	اهتَمّ ، يهتَمّ بـ

FURTHER VOCABULARY

rowing	tajdiif	تَجديف
sailing	ibHaar	إبحار
diving	ghawS/ghaTs	غَوص/غَطس
camping	takhyiim	تَخييم
horse riding	rukuub al-khayl	رُكوب الخَيل
horse racing	sibaaq al-khayl	سِباق الخَيل
shooting	rimaaya	رماية
fencing	mubaaraza	مُبارَزة
wrestling	muSaara3a	مُصارَعة

weight lifting	rafᶜ al-athqaal	رفع الأثقال
coach	mudarrib (mudarribuun/-iin)	مُدَرِّب (مُدَرِّبون/ين)
supporter	mushajjiᶜ (mushajjiᶜuun/-iin)	مُشَجِّع (مُشَجِّعون/ين)
member	ᶜuDuu (aᶜDaa')	عُضو (أعضاء)
model (e.g. model plane)	namuudhaj (namaadhij)	نَموذَج (نَماذِج)
to train, to practice	tadarraba, yatadarrab	تَدَرَّب ، يَتَدَرَّب
to go for a walk	tamashshaa, yatamashshaa	تَمَشَّى، يَتَمَشَّى
to run, to jog	jaraa, yajrii/ rakaDa, yarkuD	جري ، يجري / رَكَضَ، يركُض
to stretch	tamaddada, yatamaddad	تَمَدَّدَ، يَتَمَدَّد
to knit	taHabbaka, yataHabbak	تحَبَّكَ ، يَتَحَبَّك
to cook	Tabakha, yaTbukh	طَبَخَ ، يطبُخ
to build	banaa, yabnii	بَنى ، يَبني

 USEFUL PHRASES

What do you like to do in your free time?	ماذا تُحِبّ أن تَفعَل في وَقت الفَراغ؟
What's your favorite hobby?	ما هِيَ هوايتك المُفَضَّلة؟
Whom do you support in soccer?	أَنتَ تُشَجِّع مَن في كُرة القَدَم؟
I play the guitar and the piano.	أعزِف عَلى الجيتار والبيانو.
I'm not interested in sport.	أنا لا أهتَمّ بالرِّياضة.
I prefer reading.	أُفَضِّل المُطالَعة.
I am a member of the club.	أنا عُضو في النادي.

TOPIC 10
EXERCISES

I. Choose a word from the list below to describe each of the hobbies.

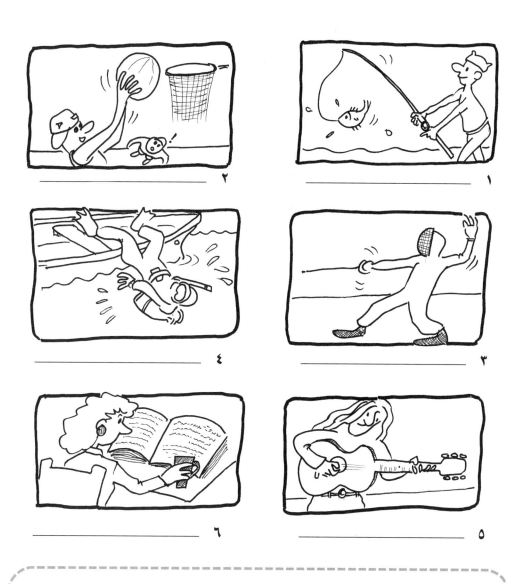

الغوص	صيد السمك	كرة السلّة
المطالعة	الموسيقى	المبارزة

2. How many of the words from the list can you find?

ي	ر	ج	و	ن	ا	ي	ب
ث	ي	م	ك	م	ن	ت	ا
ر	ا	ة	ي	ح	ر	س	م
س	ض	ق	ب	ع	ا	ل	ب
م	ة	ي	ن	غ	أ	ه	ا
ك	ط	د	م	ج	ح	ا	ر
ص	ق	ر	و	ن	م	ع	ز
ي	ب	ل	ذ	ك	م	ب	ة
ا	ل	ب	ج	ل	ل	ز	ت

sport

running

piano

player

song

drawing

dancing

model

(theater) play

fencing

skiing

3. Arrange the activities below according to where they are normally carried out.

in water	outdoors *(on land)*	indoors	in a studio

الغِناء	الغوص	مشاهدة الأفلام	سباق الخيل
السباحة	لُعبة لوحية	التخييم	التجديف
الشطرنج	الكر الطائرة	الإبحار	التصوير
ركوب الخيل	صيد السمك	رفع الأثقال	كرة السلة

4. Write a paragraph about your hobbies. Use the tables below to help you make sentences starting with the *right-hand* columns.

description (adjectives)	because	activity	I like/prefer...
مُمتِع/ مُمتِعة (enjoyable)	لأنّه (because it's [masc.])	كُرة القَدَم (soccer)	أُحبّ (I like)
مُثير/ مُثيرة (exciting)	لأنّها (because it's [fem.])	السِباحة (swimming)	أُفَضّل (I prefer)
سَهل/ سهلة (easy)		التَصوير (photography)	أهتَمّ بـ (I'm interested in)
جيِّدٌ/ جيِّدة للصحّة (good for the health)		etc. (see vocabulary)	هِوايتي المُفَضَّلة هِي (My favorite hobby is)

with	at/in	I play/do/practise
مَع أصحابي (with my friends)	في البَيت (at home)	ألعَب (I play)
مَع زُمَلائي (with my colleagues)	في النادي (in the club)	أفعَل (I do)
مَع أفراد عائلتي (with members of my family)	في الحَديقة (in the park)	أُمارس (I practice)

 REMEMBER

Arabic uses the definite article الـ al- when talking about general concepts such as hobbies. For example:

أُحبّ القِراءة. *I like reading.*

هِوايتي المُفَضَّلة هِي السِباحة. *My favorite hobby is swimming.*

Media

CORE VOCABULARY

media	wasaa'il al-iᶜlaam	وَسائِل الإعلام
communication	ittiSaal (ittiSaalaat)	إتّصال (إتّصالات)
technology	taknuuluujiyaa	تكنولوجيا
broadcast, broadcasting	idhaaᶜa (idhaaᶜaat)	إذاعة (إذاعات)
television	tiliifizyuun (tiliifizyuunaat)	تليفزيون (تليفزيونات)
radio	raadiyuu	راديو
sound	Sawt (aSwaat)	صَوت (أصوات)
tape	shariiT (ashriTa)	شَريط (أشرِطة)
disc	qurS (aqraaS)	قُرص (أقراص)
recorder	musajjil (musajjilaat)	مُسَجِّل (مُسَجِّلات)
press	SiHaafa	صِحافة
news item (pl. = news)	khabar (akhbaar)	خَبَر (أخبار)
newspaper	jariida (jaraa'id)/ SaHiifa (SuHuf)	جَريدة (جَرائد)/ صَحيفة (صُحُف)
magazine	majalla (majallaat)	مَجَلّة (مَجَلات)
article	maqaala (maqaalaat)	مَقالة (مَقالات)
computer	kumbyuutir/Haasuub	كُمبيوتر/حاسوب
keyboard	lawHat mafaatiiH	لَوحة مَفاتيح
screen	shaasha (shaashaat)	شاشة (شاشات)
printer	Taabiᶜa (Tawaabiᶜ)	طابِعة (طَوابِع)
file	milaff (milaffaat)	مِلَفّ (مِلَفّات)

internet	intarnit	إنترنت
website	mawqi^c (mawaaqi^c)	مَوقِع (مَواقِع)
channel	qanaah (qanawwat)	قَناة (قَنَوات)
telephone	haatif (hawaatif)/ tilifuun (tilifuunaat)	هاتِف (هَواتِف)/ تِلِفُون (تلفونات)
cellphone	(haatif) jawwaal/maHmuul	(هاتِف) جَوّال /مَحمول
advertisement, announcement	i^claan (i^claanaat)	إعلان (إعلانات)
program, show	barnaamaj (baraamij)	بَرنامَج (بَرامِج)
direct (broadcast, etc.)	mubaashir	مُباشِر
journalist	SuHufii (SuHufiyuun/-iin)/ SiHaafii (SiHaafiyuun/-iin)	صُحُفي (صُحُفيون /ين)/ صِحافي (صحافيون /ين)
editor	muHarrir (muHarriruun/-iin)	مُحَرِّر (مُحَرِّرون /ين)
director	mukhrij (mukhrijuun/-iin)	مُخرِج (مُخرِجون /ين)
producer	muntij (muntijuun/-iin)	مُنتِج (مُنتِجون /ين)
correspondent	muraasil (muraasiluun/-iin)	مُراسِل (مُراسِلون /ين)
photographer	muSawwir (muSawwiruun/-iin)	مُصَوِّر (مُصَوِّرون /ين)
broadcaster, announcer	mudhii^c (mudhii^cuun/-iin)	مُذيع (مُذيعون /ين)
to watch	shaahada, yushaahid	شاهَدَ ، يُشاهِد
to listen	istami^ca, yastami^c	إستَمَعَ ، يَستَمِع
to record	sajjala, yusajjil	سَجّلَ ، يُسَجّل
to print	Taba^ca, yaTba^c	طَبَعَ، يَطبَع
to publish	nashara, yanshur	نَشَرَ، يَنشُر

FURTHER VOCABULARY

press conference	mu'tamar SuHufii	مُؤتَمَر صُحُفي
editor-in-chief	ra'iis taHriir	رَئيس تَحرير
newscast, bulletin	nashrat al-akhbaar	نَشرة الأخبار
live transmission	baththh Hayy	بَثّ حَيّ
report	taqriir (taqaariir)	تَقرير (تَقارير)
news agency	wikaalat anbaa'	وِكالة أنباء

soap opera	musalasala (musalasalaat)	مُسَلسَلة (مُسَلسَلات)
episode	Halqa (Halqaat)	حَلقة (حَلقات)
satellite channel	qanaah faDaa'iyya	قناة فَضائيّة
machine	jihaaz (ajhiza)	جِهاز (أجهِزة)
World Wide Web	al-shabaka al-ᶜaalamiyya	الشَبكة العالمية
programmer	mubarmij (mubarmijuun/-iin)	مُبَرمِج (مُبَرمجون/ين)
scanner	maasiHat taSwiir	ماسِحة تصوير
downloading	taHmiil	تَحميل
log-in name	ism dukhuul	اِسم دُخول
password	kalimat sirr	كَلِمة سرّ
to produce	antaja, yuntij	أنتَجَ، يُنتِج
to show, run (program, movie)	ᶜaraDa, yaᶜruD	عَرَضَ، يَعرِض
to save, to memorize	HafiZa, yaHfaZ	حَفِظَ، يَحفَظ
to download	Hammala, yuHammil	حمَّلَ، يُحَمِّل

 USEFUL PHRASES

Dear viewers, welcome to this episode.	مُشاهِدينا الكِرام، أهلاً بِكُم في هذه الحلقة.
Dear listeners, thank you for listening ("your following") and goodbye.	مُستَمِعينا الكِرام، شكرًا على مُتابعتكم وإلى اللقاء.
Generally, I prefer the internet to newspapers.	بِشَكل عامّ، أفضّل الإنترنت على الصُحُف.
This show is very interesting/boring.	هذا البرنامج شيّق/مُمِل جدًّا.
I like watching Arabic movies.	أحِبّ أن أشاهِد الأفلام العربيّة.

EXERCISES

1. Choose a word from the list below to describe each of the pictures.

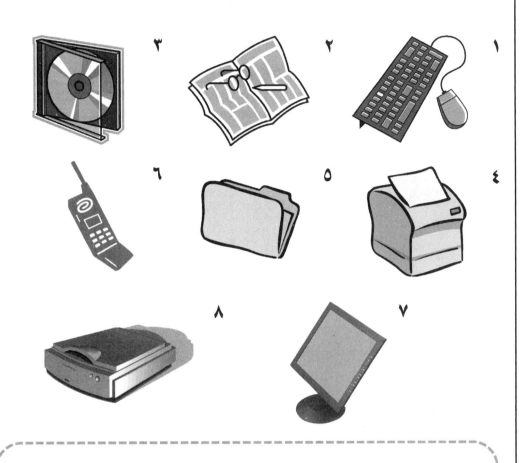

ماسحة تصوير		قرص
صحيفة		ملفّ
طابعة		هاتف محمول
شاشة		لوحة مفاتيح

2. Fill in the gaps in the sentences below using the words in the box.

١ أحبّ أن ــــــــــــ التليفزيون لكنّي لا أحبّ الإعلانات!

٢ الآن كلّ ــــــــــــ موجودة على الإنترنت.

٣ لكن جدّتي ما زالت تحبّ أن ــــــــــــ إلى الراديو.

٤ أستاذي في الجامعة يكتب ــــــــــــ لهذه المجلّة.

٥ ومن المُمكن أن تقرأ هذه المقالات في ــــــــــــ المجلّة على الإنترنت أيضًا.

موقع   أشاهد   مقالات   تستمع   الأخبار

 REMEMBER

The table on page 73 shows how to construct sentences using أنّ (that): "I prefer <u>that I</u> <u>(may) listen</u> to the radio" (see also the tip on page 37).

It is also possible to say "I prefer [the] <u>listening</u> to the radio," using a verbal noun:
أُفَضِّل الاستِماع إلى الراديو. Here are some other examples:

I like reading the papers.	أُحبّ قِراءة الصُحُف.
I prefer watching the television.	أُفَضِّل مُشاهَدة التليفزيون.
I like going to the market.	أُحبّ الذَهاب إلى السوق.

3. Write eight sentences about your preferences when it comes to how you use the media. Use the table below (reading from *right to left*) to help you.

purpose	media	preference (optional column)	how often?
للأخبار العالَمية (for international news)	أُشاهد التليفزيون ([I] watch television)	أُحبّ أن (I like to)	دائمًا (always)
للأخبار المَحلّية (for local news)	أستمع إلى الراديو ([I] listen to the radio)	أُفَضِّل أن (I prefer to)	عادةً (usually)
للأفلام (for movies)	أقرأ الصُحُف ([I] read the papers)		أحيانًا (sometimes)
للطقس (for the weather)	أتصفَّح الإنترنت ([I] surf the internet)		في مُعظَم الأحيان (mostly)
للتَّسلية (for entertainment)	أستَخدِم الهاتف المَحمول ([I] use the mobile phone)		نادرًا ما (rarely)

Weather and environment

CORE VOCABULARY

weather	Taqs	طَقس
environment	bii'a	بيئة
nature	Tabii'a	طَبيعة
atmosphere, weather	jaw (ajwaa')	جَو (أجواء)
climate	munaakh (munaakhaat)	مُناخ (مُناخات)
season	faSl (fuSuul)	فَصل (فُصول)
spring	ar-rabii'	الرَبيع
summer	aS-Sayf	الصَيف
autumn, fall	al-khariif	الخَريف
winter	ash-shitaa'	الشِتاء
heat	Haraara	حَرارة
hot	Haarr/saakhin	حارّ/ ساخِن
clear, fine	SaHw	صَحو
temperature	darajat al-Haraara	دَرَجة الحَرارة
cold (noun)	bard/buruuda	بَرد/بُرودة
cold (adjective)	baarid	بارِد
warm	daafi'	دافِئ
moderate, temperate	mu'tadil	مُعتَدِل
humidity	ruTuuba	رُطوبة
cloud	saHaaba (suHub)	سَحابة (سُحُب)
rain	maTar	مَطر

ice, snow	thalj	ثَلج
sunny	mushmis	مُشمِس
cloudy	ghaa'im	غائِم
rainy	mumTir	مُمطِر
icy, snowy	muthlij	مُثلِج
sky	samaa' (samaawaat)	سَماء (سماوات)
earth, land	arD (araaDin)	أرض (أراضٍ)
sun	shams	شَمس
moon	qamar (aqmaar)	قَمَر (أقمار)
water	maa' (miyaah)	ماء (مياه)
air	hawaa'	هَواء
earth, dust	turaab (atriba)	تُراب (أتربة)
fire	naar	نار (نيران)
wind	riiH	ريح (رياح)
storm	ᶜaaSifa (ᶜawaaSif)	عاصِفة (عَواصِف)
pollution	talawwuth	تَلَوُّث
cause, reason	sabab (asbaab)	سَبَب (أسباب)
to cause	sabbaba, yusabbib	سَبّبَ ، يُسَبّب
to protect	Hamaa, yaHmii	حَمى، يَحمي

FURTHER VOCABULARY

fog	Dabaab	ضَباب
flood	fayDaan	فَيضان
earthquake	zilzaal (zalaazil)	زِلزال (زلازِل)
tornado	iᶜSaar (iᶜSaaraat)	إعصار
protection	Himaaya	حِماية
planet	kawkab (kawaakib)	كَوكَب (كَواكِب)
the Globe, the Earth	al-kura al-arDiyya	الكُرة الأرضيّة
natural	Tabiiᶜii	طَبيعيّ
organic	ᶜuDwii	عُضويّ

harm	Darar	ضَرَر
poisonous	saamm	سامّ
lightening	barq	بَرق
sandstorm	ᶜaaSifa ramliyya	عاصفة رَمليّة
snowstorm	ᶜaaSifa thaljiyya	عاصفة ثَلجيّة
heat wave	mawja haarra	مَوجة حارّة
shade	Zill	ظِلّ
wet	muballal	مُبَلَّل
dry	jaaff	جافّ
drought	qaHT/jafaaf	قَحط/جَفاف
to pollute	lawwatha, yulawwith	لَوَّثَ، يُلَوّث
to blow (the wind)	habba, yahibb	هَبَّ، يَهِبّ

 USEFUL PHRASES

How's the weather today?	كَيف حالة الجَو اليَوم؟
The weather is cold/hot/sunny/snowy.	الجَو بارِد/حارّ/مُشمِس/مُثلِج.
Snow is falling.	الثَلج يَتَساقَط.
Wind is blowing.	الريح تَهِبّ.
The temperature is high/low.	دَرَجة الحَرارة عالية/مُنخَفِضة.
The Earth's temperature has risen greatly in recent years.	حَرارة الأرض اِرتَفَعَت كَثيرًا في السَنَوات الأخيرة.
Modern factories are one of the causes of pollution.	المَصانع الحَديثة سَبَب من أسباب التَلَوُّث.

EXERCISES

---

1. Complete the crossword using the clues provided (see Tip on page 16).

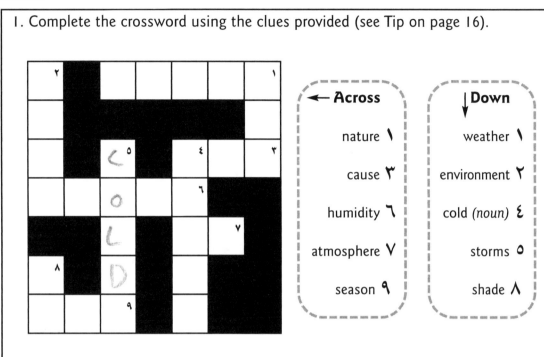

← **Across**

nature ١

cause ٣

humidity ٦

atmosphere ٧

season ٩

↓ **Down**

weather ١

environment ٢

cold (noun) ٤

storms ٥

shade ٨

---

2. Put the words in order, from the hottest to the coldest.

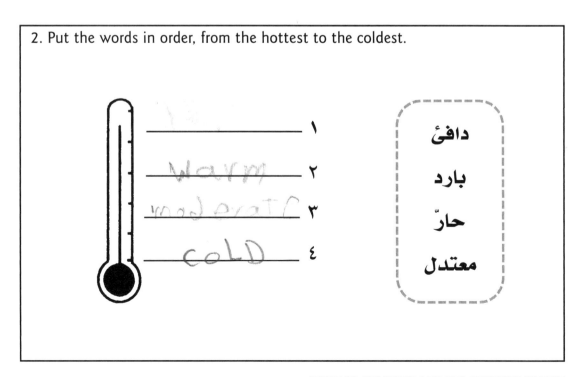

١ ‎——————

٢ Warm

٣ moderate

٤ COLD

دافئ

بارد

حارّ

معتدل

3. Label the natural features in each picture, and then say what the weather is like. The words you need are all in the main vocabulary lists.

_____ ٢

شمس

_____ الجو/الطقس ١

_____ ٤

_____ ٣

4. Describe the weather for this week, using the table below to help you.

level	temperature/ humidity	description	weather	time of day	day of the week
عالية (high)	ودَرَجة الحَرارة (and the temperature is...)	مُشمِس (sunny)	الجو/الطقس... (the weather is...)	في الصَّباح (in the morning)	يوم الأحَد (Sunday)
مُعتَدِلة (moderate)	والرُطوبة (and the humidity is...)	صَحو (fine)		بَعد الظُّهر (in the afternoon)	يوم الاثنَين (Monday)
مُنخَفِضة (low)		مُمطِر (rainy)		في المَساء (in the evening)	يوم الثلاثاء (Tuesday)
		مُثلِج (snowy)		في اللَيل (at night)	يوم الأربعاء (Wednesday)
		حارّ (hot)			يوم الخَميس (Thursday)
		بارِد (cold)			يوم الجُمعة (Friday)
		etc. (see vocabulary)			يوم السَبت (Saturday)

 REMEMBER

It is easy to convert the present tense sentences above into the past or the future. For the past, you use كان/كانت ("was") and for the future you use سيَكون/ستَكون ("will be"). In both cases, the adjective takes on the -an ending, which results in an additional alif on nouns not ending in taa' marbuuTa.

Present	⟶	Past	⟶	Future
الجو بارد.		كانَ الجو بارِدًا.		سيَكون الجو بارِدًا.
الرطوبة عالية.		كانَت الرطوبة عالية.		ستَكون الرطوبة عالية.

TOPIC 13

Local Area

CORE VOCABULARY

region	minTaqa (manaaTiq)	مِنطَقة (مَناطِق)
place	makaan (amaakin)	مَكان (أماكِن)
city	madiina (mudun)	مَدينة (مُدُن)
countryside	riif (aryaaf)	ريف (أرياف)
village	qarya (quran)	قَرية (قُرًى)
street	shaariᶜ (shawaariᶜ)	شارِع (شَوارِع)
road, way	Tariiq (Turuq)	طَريق (طُرُق)
traffic	muruur	مُرور
block (*offices, apartments, etc.*)	ᶜimaara (ᶜimaaraat)	عِمارة (عِمارات)
building	mabnaa (mabaanin)	مَبنى (مَبانٍ)
town hall	mabnaa al-baladiyya	مَبنى البَلَديّة
school	madrasa (madaaris)	مَدرسة (مَدارِس)
hotel	funduq (fanaadiq)	فُندُق (فَنادِق)
restaurant	maTᶜam (maTaaᶜim)	مَطعَم (مَطاعِم)
café, coffee shop	maqhaa (maqaahin)	مَقهى (مَقاهٍ)
pharmacy	Saydaliyya (Saydaliyyaat)	صَيدَليّة (صَيدَليّات)
bank	bank (bunuuk)/ maSraf (maSaarif)	بَنك (بُنُوك)/ مَصرِف (مَصارِف)
police station	markaz (maraakiz) shurTa	مَركَز (مَراكِز) شُرطة
gas station	maHaTTat (maHaTTaat) banziin	مَحطّة (مَحطّات) بَنزين
beach	shaaTi' (shawaaTi')	شاطِئ (شَواطِئ)

mosque	masjid (masaajid)/ jaami⁣ᶜ (jawaamiᶜ)	مَسجِد (مَساجِد)/ جامِع (جوامِع)
church	kaniisa (kanaa'is)	كَنيسة (كَنائِس)
club	naadin (nawaadin)	نادٍ (نوادٍ)
park, garden	Hadiiqa (Hadaa'iq)	حَديقة (حَدائِق)
library, bookstore	maktaba (makaatib)	مكتَبة (مَكتَبات)
downtown	wasaT al-madiina	وَسَط المدينة
post office	maktab (makaatib) al-bariid	مكتَب (مَكاتِب) البَريد
movie theater	siinimaa	سينِما
theater	masraH (masaariH)	مَسرَح (مَسارِح)
bridge	jisr (jusuur)	جِسر (جُسور)
palace	qaSr (quSuur)	قَصر (قُصور)
farm	mazraᶜa (mazaariᶜ)	مَزرَعة (مَزارِع)
mountain	jabal (jibaal)	جَبَل (جِبال)
river	nahr (anhaar)	نَهر (أنهار)
north	shamaal	شمال
west	gharb	غَرب
south	januub	جَنوب
east	sharq	شَرق
to roam around	tajawwala, yatajawwal	تَجَوَّل ، يَتَجَوَّل
to get lost	taaha, yatuuh	تاه، يَتوه

FURTHER VOCABULARY

path	madaqq (madaqqaat)	مَدَقّ (مَدَقّات)
temple	maᶜbad (maᶜaabid)	مَعبَد (مَعابِد)
synagogue	maᶜbad yahuudii	مَعبَد يَهودي
skyscraper	naaTiHat (naaTiHaat) saHaab	ناطِحة (ناطِحات) سَحاب
congestion	izdiHaam	اِزدِحام
district, quarter	Hayy (aHyaa')	حَيّ (أحياء)
suburb	DaaHiya (DawaaHii)	ضاحية (ضَواحٍ)

sport center	markaz (maraakiz) riyaaDii	مَركَز (مَراكِز) رياضيّ
garage	garaaj (garaajaat)	جَراج (جَراجات)
corner	naaSiya (nawaaSin)	ناصية (نواصٍ)
forest	ghaaba (ghaabaat)	غابة (غابات)
hill	tall (tilaal)	تَلّ (تِلال)
to park (a vehicle)	awqafa, yuuqif	أوقَفَ ، يوقِف
to establish, to found	assasa, yu'assis	أسَّسَ ، يُؤَسِّس

 USEFUL PHRASES

Excuse me, where's the police station?	لو سَمَحت، أين مَركَز الشُّرطة؟
Is this the way to the Old City?	هل هذا هو الطريق إلى المدينة القديمة؟
Go straight ahead.	امشِ عَلى طول .
Take the first street on the right/left.	خُذ أوّل شارِع عَلى اليَمين /اليَسار
Is there a bank near here?	هل يُوجَد بنك قَريب من هنا؟
The park is located in front of the royal palace.	تَقَع الحَديقة أمام القَصر المَلَكيّ .

I. Match the words below with the numbered features in the town.

عمارة   مسجد

كنيسة   شارع

بنك/مصرف   فندق

مقهى   مطعم

2. How many of the words can you find in the word search?

ع	ض	ص	ق	م	ف	غ	ع	ه	ق	ي	ر	ط	ض
م	ث	ق	ي	ر	ط	ه	خ	ح	ج	د	د	ش	س
ا	م	ن	ت	و	ا	ة	ق	ط	ن	م	ل	ب	ج
ر	ط	ف	ي	ر	ش	س	ر	ي	ب	د	ل	ل	ت
ة	لا	ر	ؤ	ء	ئ	ك	ي	ط	ك	ي	م	ا	ت
ظ	ز	و	ة	لا	لا	ر	ة	ب	ق	ن	ا	ك	م
ن	م	ا	ح	د	ز	ا	ب	ر	غ	ة	د	ي	ش

region	traffic	countryside	congestion
road	village	hill	west
city	place	block	mountain

REMEMBER

These are two very useful verbs for describing position. Use them in the following way:

"it is situated" (for towns and cities)   يَقَع/تَقَع

"it is found" (for objects and features)   يوجَد/توجَد

3. Here is a description of the area where someone lives:

أسكُن في مَدينة صغيرة اسمها ... تقع في الغرب قريبة من ...

هناك محلات جميلة وأسواق كثيرة في وسط المدينة.

توجد ثلاث مدارس ومكتبة جديدة . هناك سينما ولكن ليس هناك مسرح.

في الضواحي هناك حديقة كبيرة فيها نهر ويوجد في الريف قصر قديم.

Now write a similar paragraph about where you live. Use the following phrases to help you:

- I live in a town/village called...   أسكُن في مَدينة/قَرية اسمها ...

- near to …   قَريب من ...

- It is situated in …   تقع في ...

- There is/are… but there isn't/aren't...   هُناك ... ولكن لَيس هُناك ...

- … can be found (masc./fem.)   يوجد/ توجد ...

_____

_____

_____

_____

_____

_____

TOPIC 14

Travel and tourism

CORE VOCABULARY

travel	safar	سَفَر
tourism	siyaaHa	سياحة
journey, trip	riHla (riHlaat)	رِحلة (رِحلات)
visit	ziyaara (ziyaaraat)	زيارة (زيارات)
country	balad (bilaad/buldaan)	بَلَد (بِلاد/بُلدان)
traveler	musaafir (musaafiruun/-iin)	مُسافِر (مُسافِرون/ين)
car	sayyaara (sayyaaraat)	سَيّارة (سَيّارات)
taxi	taaksii/sayyaarat ujra	تاكسي/سَيّارة أُجرة
bicycle	darraja (darrajaat)	دَرّاجة (دَرّاجات)
train	qiTaar (qiTaaraat)	قِطار (قِطارات)
plane	Taai'ira (Taai'iraat)	طائِرة (طائِرات)
boat	qaarib (qawaarib)	قارِب (قَوارِب)
ship	safiina (sufun)	سَفينة (سُفُن)
bus	baaS (baaSaat)/ uutuubiis (uutuubiisaat)	باص (باصات)/ أوتوبيس (أوتوبيسات)
airport	maTaar (maTaaraat)	مَطار (مطارات)
stop *(bus, train, etc.)*	mawqif (mawaaqif)	مَوقِف (مواقِف)
station	maHaTTa (maHaTTaat)	مَحَطّة (مَحَطّات)
port, harbor	miinaa' (mawaanin)	ميناء (موانٍ)
passport	jawaaz (jawaazaat) as-safar	جَواز (جَوازات) السَّفَر
visa	ta'shiira (ta'shiiraat)	تَأشيرة (تَأشيرات)

ticket	tadhkira (tadhaakir)	تَذكِرة (تَذاكِر)
one-way	dhahaab	ذَهاب
roundtrip	dhahaab wa-iiyaab/wa-ᶜawda	ذَهاب وإياب/وعَودة
sea	baHr (biHaar)	بَحر (بِحار)
seaside, shore	shaaTi' (shawaaTi')	شاطِئ (شَواطِئ)
baggage	amtiᶜa	أمتِعة
camera	aalat taSwiir/kaamiiraa	آلة تَصوير/كاميرا
postcard	biTaaqa bariidiyya	بِطاقة بَريديّة
fast	sariiᶜ	سَريع
slow	baTii'	بَطيء
straight on	ᶜalaa Tuul	عَلى طول
before	qabla	قَبلَ
after	baᶜda	بَعدَ
to go	dhahaba, yadh-hab	ذَهَبَ ، يَذهَب
to walk	mashaa, yamshii	مَشى ، يَمشي
to return	rajaᶜa, yarjaᶜ/ ᶜaadu, yaᶜuud	رَجعَ ، يَرجَع/ عاد ، يعود
to travel	saafara, yusaafir	سافَرَ ، يُسافِر
to ride, to catch, to board	rakiba, yarkab	رَكِبَ ، يركَب
to spend (time)	qaDaa, yaqDii	قَضى ، يَقضي
to arrive	waSala, yaSil	وَصلَ ، يَصِل

FURTHER VOCABULARY

pilgrimage	Hajj	حَجّ
pilgrim	Haaj (Hujjaaj)	حاجّ (حُجّاج)
the holy land	al-araaDii al-muqaddasa	الأراضي المُقَدّسة
public transportation	al-naql al-ᶜaam	النَقل العام
means of transportation	wasiilat (wasaa'il) naql	وَسيلة (وَسائل) نَقل
seat	maqᶜad (maqaaᶜid)	مقعَد (مقاعِد)
crossroad	muftaraq Turuq	مُفترَق طُرُق

traffic lights	ishaaraat al-muruur	إشارات المُرور
railroad	sikkat al-Hadiid	سكّة الحَديد
campsite	mukhayyam (mukhayyamaat)	مُخَيَّم (مُخَيَّمات)
tunnel	nafaq (anfaaq)	نَفَق (أنفاق)
subway train	qiTaar anfaaq	قطار أنفاق
bus, coach	Haafila (Hawaafil)	حافِلة (حَوافِل)
on time	fil-miiᶜaad	في الميعاد
abroad	al-khaarij	الخارِج
youth hostel	bayt shabaab	بَيت شَباب
to take off	aqlaᶜa, yuqliᶜ	أقلَعَ ، يُقلِع
to land	habaTa, yahbuT	هَبَطَ ، يهبُط
to go down; to stay	nazala, yanzil	نَزَلَ ، ينزِل
to cross	ᶜabara, yaᶜbur	عَبَرَ ، يعبُر
to hurry	istaᶜjala, yastaᶜjil	استَعجَل ، يَستَعجِل
to receive	istaqbala, yastaqbil	استَقبَلَ ، يَستَقبِل
to welcome	raHHaba, yuraHHib	رَحَّبَ ، يُرَحِّب

USEFUL PHRASES

Have a nice stay!	إقامة سَعيدة!
Have a nice trip!	رِحلة سَعيدة!
We spent six days in Cairo.	قَضَينا سِتّة أيام في القاهرة.
We reserved a room overlooking the sea.	حَجَزنا غُرفة تُطِلّ على البحر.
We want to reserve seats on the train.	نُريد أن نَحجُز مقاعِد في القِطار.
Is there airconditioning?	هَل هُناك تَكييف؟

EXERCISES

1. Find words in the vocabulary list to describe the pictures below.

_____ ٢

_____ ١

_____ ٤

_____ ٣

_____ ٦

_____ ٥

REMEMBER

To say "by" when talking about transportation Arabic uses بالـ... bil-:

by plane/by bus/by car

بالطائرة/بالباص/بالسيّارة

2. Complete the crossword using the clues provided (see tip on page 16).

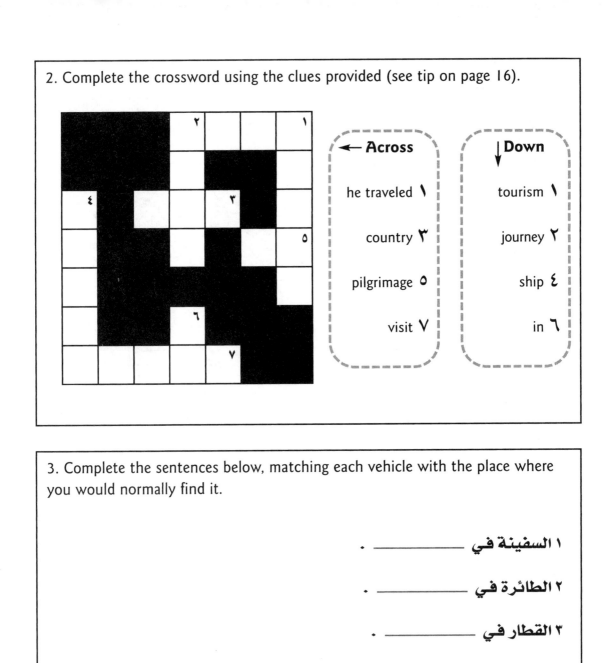

← **Across**

he traveled ١

country ٣

pilgrimage ٥

visit ٧

↓ **Down**

tourism ١

journey ٢

ship ٤

in ٦

3. Complete the sentences below, matching each vehicle with the place where you would normally find it.

١ السفينة في _____ .

٢ الطائرة في _____ .

٣ القطار في _____ .

٤ الباص في _____ .

الموقف   الميناء   المحطّة   المطار

4. You are planning a trip involving several stops, and using different modes of transportation. Write a paragraph about the trip, using the future tense, with the help of the table below (starting with the *right-hand* column).

from/to	transportation	verb	travel	sequence
مِن ... (from …)	الباص ([the] bus)	سَأذهَب بـِ (I will go by)	سَأُسافِر إلى ... (I will travel to …)	أوَّلاً (firstly)
إلى ... (to …)	القطار ([the] train)	سَأركب (I will catch)	سنُسافِر إلى ... (we will travel to …)	ثانيًا (secondly)
	الطائرة ([the] plane)	سنذهب بـِ (we will go by)		ثالثًا (thirdly)
	السفينة ([the] ship)	سنَركب (we will catch)		ثُمَّ (then)
	السيّارة ([the] car)			بَعدَ ذلك (after that)
	الدرّاجة ([the] bicycle)			

_____

_____

_____

_____

_____

TOPIC 15

Education

CORE VOCABULARY

student (college)	Taalib (Tullaab, Talaba)	طالِب (طُلّاب، طَلَبة)
student (school)	tilmiidh (talaamiidh)	تِلميذ (تَلاميذ)
teacher	muᶜallim (muᶜallimuun/-iin)/ mudarris (mudarrisuun/-iin)	مُعَلِّم (مُعَلِّمون/ين)/ مُدَرِّس (مُدَرِّسون/ين)
professor, teacher	ustaadh (asaatidha)	أُستاذ (أَساتِذة)
primary school	madrasa ibtidaa'iyya	مَدرَسة اِبتِدائِيّة
junior high school	madrasa iᶜdaadiyya	مَدرَسة إعدادِيّة
high school	madrasa thaanawiyya	مَدرَسة ثانَوِيّة
college, faculty	kulliya (kulliyaa)	كُلِّية (كُلِّيات)
university	jaamiᶜa (jaamiᶜaat)	جامِعة (جامِعات)
class, classroom	Saff (Sufuuf)	صَفّ (صُفوف)
semester, class	faSl (fuSuul)	فَصل (فُصول)
lesson	dars (duruus)	دَرس (دُروس)
homework	waajib madrasii	واجِب مَدرَسيّ
book	kitaab (kutub)	كِتاب (كُتُب)
exercise book	kurraasa (kurraasaat)	كُرّاسة (كُرّاسات)
pen	qalam (aqlaam)	قَلَم (أقلام)
pencil	qalam raSaaS	قَلَم رَصاص
eraser	maHHaaya (maHHaayaat)	مَحّاية (مَحّايات)
pencil sharpener	barraaya (barraayaat)	بَرّاية (بَرّايات)
ruler	misTara (masaaTir)	مِسطَرة (مَساطِر)

notebook	daftar (dafaatir)	دَفتَر (دَفاتر)
dictionary	qaamuus (qawaamiis)	قاموس (قَواميس)
letter (of the alphabet)	Harf (Huruuf)	حَرف (حُروف)
number	raqam (arqaam)	رَقَم (أرقام)
question	su'aal (as'ila)	سُؤال (أسئلة)
answer	ijaaba (ijaabaat)	إجابة (إجابات)
exam	imtiHaan (imtiHaanaat)	امتِحان (امتِحانات)
mathematics	riyaaDiyaat	رياضيّات
literature	adab (aadaab)	أَدَب (آداب)
English language	al-lugha al-ingliiziyya	اللّغة الإنجليزيّة
Arabic language	al-lugha al-ᶜarabiyya	اللّغة العَرَبيّة
history	taariikh	تاريخ
geography	jughraafiyaa	جُغرافيا
science	ᶜuluum	عُلوم
biology	ᶜilm al-aHyaa'	علم الأحياء
chemistry	ᶜilm al-kiimiyaa'	علم الكيمياء
physics	ᶜilm al-fiiziiyaa'	علم الفيزياء
to study	darasa, yadrus	دَرَسَ ، يَدرُس
to teach	darrasa, yudarris/ ᶜallama, yuᶜallim	دَرَّسَ ، يُدَرِّس / عَلَّمَ ، يُعَلِّم
to learn	taᶜallam, yataᶜallam	تَعَلَّمَ ، يَتَعَلَّم

FURTHER VOCABULARY

principal	naaZir (nuZZaar)	ناظِر (نُظّار)
school administration	idaarat al-madrasa	إدارة المدرسة
administrative worker	mas'uul al-idaara	مَسؤول الإدارة
registration	tasjiil	تَسجيل
admissions office	maktab al-qubuul	مكتب القُبول
period, lesson	HiSSa (HiSaS)	حِصّة (حِصَص)
schedule	jadwal (jadaawil)	جَدوَل (جَداول)

page	SafHa (safaHaat)	صَفحة (صَفَحات)
ink	Hibr	حِبر
scholarship	minHa	مِنحة
board	sabbuura (sabbuuraat)	سَبّورة (سَبّورات)
chalk	Tabaashiir	طباشير
school uniform	zii madrasii	زِيّ مدرسيّ
private/state school	madrasa khaaSSa/ᶜaamma	مدرسة خاصّة/عامّة
nursery	rawDa/HaDaana	روضة/حَضانة
psychology	ᶜilm an-nafs	عِلم النَّفس
sociology	ᶜilm al-ijtimaaᶜ	عِلم الاجتماع
economics	ᶜilm al-iqtiSaad	عِلم الاقتصاد
to review	raajaᶜa, yuraajiᶜ	راجِع، يُراجِع
to ask	sa'ala, yas'al	سألَ، يَسأل
to answer	ajaaba, yujiib	أجابَ، يُجيب
to enroll	iltaHaqa, yaltaHiq bi	التَحَقَ، يَلتَحِق بِـ
to look for, to search	baHatha, yabHath ᶜan	بَحثَ، يَبحَث عَن
to memorize	HafaZa, yaHfaZ	حفَظَ، يَحفَظ

 USEFUL PHRASES

Raise (m) your hand.	اِرفَع يَدك.
Take out (f) your pen.	أخرِجي قَلَمك.
Open (pl) your books.	اِفتَحوا كُتُبكُم.
Do you (pl) have any questions?	هَل عِندكُم أيّ أسئلة؟

(See also list of instructions on page 105.)

TOPIC 15
EXERCISES

1. Choose a word from the vocabulary list to describe each of the pictures.

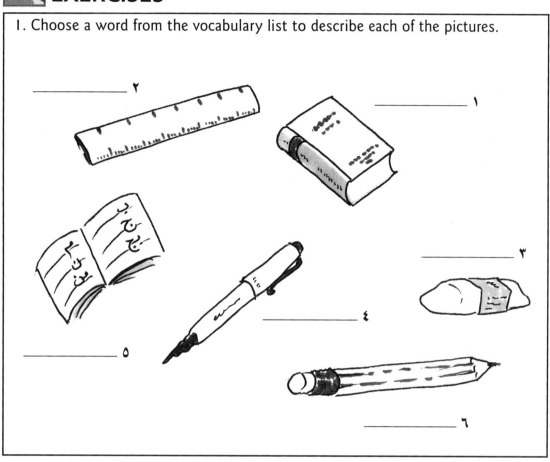

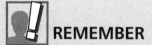

REMEMBER

Essentially, the imperative for giving instructions works like this:

	Masculine singular	Feminine singular	Plural
open!	اِفتَح!	اِفتَحي!	اِفتَحوا!
write!	اُكتُب!	اُكتُبي!	اُكتُبوا!

Remember to add ي (-ii) for the feminine and وا (-uu) for the plural. The final *alif* of the plural is silent.

2. Write the plurals of these words next to the singular.

١ مُدَرّس ــــــــــــ   ٥ سُؤال ــــــــــــ

٢ جامعة ــــــــــــ   ٦ رَقْم ــــــــــــ

٣ فَصل ــــــــــــ   ٧ مِسطَرة ــــــــــــ

٤ كِتاب ــــــــــــ   ٨ دَفتَر ــــــــــــ

3. Fill in the blanks with the appropriate verb from the box below.

١ أنا طالب و ــــــــــــ الأدب العربيّ في الجامعة.

٢ سأسافر إلى فَرَنسا لـ ــــــــــــ اللغة الفَرَنسيّة.

٣ أنا أستاذ في كليّة الآداب و ــــــــــــ التاريخ.

٤ ــــــــــــ للامتِحانات في مايو.

٥ ــــــــــــ كتابكِ صَفحة ٦٥.

٦ أبي ــــــــــــ القُرآن في طُفولته.

٧ التلامذة ــــــــــــ عن إجابة السؤال على الانتَرنَت.

٨ هل أنتَ ــــــــــــ اللغة الفَرَنسيّة أيضًا في المدرسة؟

يبحثون	أتعلّم	تتعلّم	أدرُس
اِفتحي	أدرُس	أراجع	حفظ

4. Look at Nabil's schedule for Sunday and Monday. Make sentences about what he studies in every class, following the example. Then try to make some similar sentences about the subjects you and/or your family and friends are studying. (See page 49 for help on expressing times of the day in Arabic.)

	الساعة ٨ إلى الساعة ٩٫٣٠	الساعة ٩٫٤٥ إلى الساعة ١١٫١٥	الساعة ١١٫٣٠ إلى الساعة ١	الساعة ٢ إلى الساعة ٣٫٣٠
يوم الأحد	التاريخ	الجغرافيا	العربية	الرياضيات
يوم الاثنين	الإنجليزية	التاريخ	علم الأحياء	الفيزياء

يوم الأحد يدرس نبيل التاريخ من الساعة الثامنة إلى الساعة التاسعة والنصف.

_____

_____

_____

_____

_____

_____

Work

CORE VOCABULARY

work	ʿamal (aʿmaal)/ shughl (ashghaal)	عَمَل (أعمال)/ شُغْل (أشغال)
profession	mihna (mihan)	مِهنة (مِهَن)
job, position	waZiifa (waZaa'if)	وَظيفة (وَظائف)
company	sharika (sharikaat)	شَرِكة (شَرِكات)
branch	farʿ (furuuʿ)	فَرع (فُروع)
office	maktab (makaatib)	مَكتَب (مَكاتِب)
experience	khibra	خِبرة
trade	tijaara	تِجارة
manager, director	mudiir (mudaraa')	مُدير (مُدَراء)
worker	ʿaamil (ʿummaal)	عامِل (عُمّال)
secretary	sikritayra (sikritayraat)	سِكرِتَيرة (سِكرِتَيرات)
employee, government employee	muwaZZaf (muwaZZafuun/iin)	مُوَظَّف (مُوَظَّفون/ين)
expert	khabiir (khubaraa')	خَبير (خُبَراء)
specialist	mutakhaSSiS (mutakhaSSiSuun/-iin)	مُتخَصِّص (مُتخَصِّصون/ين)
businessman	rajul (rijaal) aʿmaal	رَجُل (رِجال) أعمال
businesswoman	sayyida (sayyidaat) aʿmaal	سَيِّدة (سَيِّدات) أعمال
researcher	baaHith (baaHithuun/-iin)	باحِث (باحِثون/ين)
trader	taajir (tujjaar)	تاجِر (تُجّار)
lawyer	muHaamin (muHaamuun/-iin)	مُحامٍ (مُحامون/ين)

judge	qaaDin (quDaah)	قاضٍ (قُضَاة)
engineer	muhandis (muhandisuun/-iin)	مُهَندِس (مُهَندِسون/ين)
pilot	Tayyaar (Tayyaaruun/-iin)	طَيّار (طَيّارون/ين)
driver	saa'iq (saa'iquun/-iin)	سائِق (سائقون/ين)
mechanic	miikaniikii (miikaniikiyuun/-iin)	ميكانيكي (ميكانيكيون/ين)
electrician	kahrabaa'ii (kahrabaa'iyuun/-iin)	كَهرَبائي (كَهرَبائيون/ين)
plumber	sabbaak (sabbaakuun/-iin)	سَبّاك (سَبّاكون/ين)
cook	Tabbaakh (Tabbaakhuun/-iin)	طَبّاخ (طَبّاخون/ين)
confectioner	Halwaanii (Halwaaniyuun/-iin)	حَلَواني (حَلَوانيون/ين)
barber	Hallaq (Hallaquun/-iin)	حَلاق (حَلاقون/ين)
florist	baa'iᶜ zuhuur (baaᶜa zuhuur)	بائع زُهُور (باعة زُهُور)
farmer	muzaariᶜ (muzaariᶜuun/-iin)	مُزارِع (مُزارِعون/ين)
artist	fannaan (fannaanuun/-iin)	فَنّان (فَنّانون/ين)
unemployment	baTaala	بَطالة
unemployed	aaTil	عاطِل
retirement	taqaaᶜud	تَقاعُد
retired	mutaqaaᶜid	مُتقاعد
salary	raatib (rawaatib)	راتِب (رواتِب)
(working) hours	dawaam	دوام
to work	ᶜamila, yaᶜmal	عَمِلَ ، يَعمَل
to employ	waZZafa, yuwaZZif	وَظَّفَ ، يُوَظّف

FURTHER VOCABULARY

ambitious	TamuuH	طَموح
gifted	mawhuub	مَوهوب
project	mashruuᶜ (mashaariiᶜ)	مَشروع (مشاريع)
plan	khiTTa (khiTaT)	خِطّة (خِطَط)
future	mustaqbal	مُستَقبَل

organization	munaZZama (munaZZamaat)	مُنَظّمة (مُنَظّمات)
commodity	biDaaᶜa (baDaa'iᶜ)	بِضاعة (بَضائِع)
job vacancy	waZiifa shaaghira	وَظيفة شاغِرة
employer, boss	rabb ᶜamal (arbaab aᶜmaal)	رَبّ عَمَل (أرباب أعمال)
consultant	istishaarii (istishaariyuun/-iin)	إستِشاريّ (إستِشاريّون/ين)
agent, representative	wakiil (wukalaa')	وَكيل (وُكَلاء)
accountant	muHaasib (muHaasibuun/-iin)	مُحاسِب (مُحاسِبون/ين)
translator	mutarjim (mutarjimuun/-iin)	مُتَرجِم (مُتَرجِمون/ين)
servant	khaadim (khadam)	خادِم (خَدَم)
pension	maaᶜash taqaaᶜud	مَعاش تقاعُد
part-time	dawaam juz'ii	دَوام جُزئي
full-time	dawaam kaamil	دَوام كامِل
exploitation	istighlaal	إستِغلال
insurance	ta'miin	تأمين
to succeed	najaHa, yanjaH	نَجَحَ ، يَنجَح
to fail	fashala, yafshal	فَشَلَ ، يَفشَل
to sack, to fire	faSala, yafSil	فَصَلَ ، يَفصِل
to earn	kasaba, yaksib	كَسَبَ ، يكسِب
to make, to manufacture	Sanaᶜa, yaSnaᶜ	صَنَعَ ، يصنَع
to pay	dafaᶜa, yadfaᶜ	دَفَعَ ، يدفَع
to run, to manage	adaara, yudiir	أدارَ ، يُدير

 # USEFUL PHRASES

What does your father/mother do?	ماذا يَعمل والِدك؟ / ماذا تَعمل والِدتك؟
Do you have a plan for the future?	هل عِندك خِطّة لِلمستقبل؟
I want to be become an engineer.	أُريد أن أُصبِح مُهَندِسًا.
I want to work in a big company.	أُريد أن أعمل في شركة كبيرة.
Currently, I am looking for work.	حاليًا أنا أبحث عن العمل.
I work part-time every Sunday.	أعمل في دَوام جُزئي كُلّ يوم أحد.

EXERCISES

1. Choose a word from the vocabulary list to describe each of the professions. Remember to add ة for the feminine.

2. Circle the odd-one-out in each set of words.

شغل	وظيفة	فنّان	١ عمل
بطالة	منظّمة	شركة	٢ مكتب
مهندس	حلواني	كهربائي	٣ سبّاك
باحثة	مهنة	متخصّصة	٤ خبيرة
خادم	متخصّص	ربّ عمل	٥ مدير
تأمين	راتب	معاش تعاقد	٦ قاضٍ

3. Fill in the blanks with the appropriate verb, changing it to agree with the subject if necessary.

١ والدتي _____ في بنك كبير في لندن.

٢ ابني محامٍ وراتبه مُمتاز. هو _____ أكثر منّي.

٣ أرباب الأعمال _____ الرواتب ومعاشات التقاعد.

٤ هي أكبر شركة في المدينة و _____ نصف السكان.

٥ يَجِب أن _____ المدير بعض العُمّال بعد أن _____ المشروع.

يدفع	يعمل	يكسب
يفصل	فشل	يوظّف

4. Talk about your profession and/or the professions of your family and friends, with the help of the table below.

description	place	in/for	profession	who
كبير(ة) (big)	شركة (a company)	في (in)	باحث/باحثة (a researcher)	أنا (I)
صغير(ة) (small)	بنك (a bank)	لـ (for)	مهندس/مهندسة (an engineer)	أخي (my brother)
جديد(ة) (new)	منظّمة (an organization)		etc. (see vocabulary)	أُختي (my sister)
قديم(ة) (old)	مدرسة (a school)		أعمل ([I] work)	والدي (my father)
أجنَبي(ة) (foreign)	مصنع (a factory)		يعمل ([he] works)	والدتي (my mother)
مَحلّي(ة) (local)	etc. (see vocabulary)		تعمل ([she] works)	صديقي/صديقتي (my friend)

 REMEMBER

In this topic, you have met two "weak" nouns: قاض (judge) and مُحام (lawyer). The ending of weak nouns changes depending on the situation

Formal (indefinite)	**Formal** (definite)	**Colloquial**
قاض qaaDin	القاضي qaaDii	قاضي qaaDii
مُحام muHaamin	المحامي muHaamii	مُحامي muHaamii

Other weak words include: ماض (past), واد (valley), ناد (club), and غال (expensive/an expensive object).

Examination tips and instructions in Arabic

PREPARING FOR EXAMINATIONS

Once you have worked your way through this book, you will have the solid foundation in Arabic vocabulary that you need to tackle examinations. Each examination has its own demands, so it is best to know what they are and tailor your preparation according to them.

1   Obtain examples of past papers and *go through them systematically*. Make a note of words that occur frequently. It may be that you already know most of the words, but watch out for new ones and make sure you learn them. Many public examinations reuse a lot of vocabulary, so being familiar with the content of past papers is a sound strategy.

2   There are some things you might need to learn in addition to what you find in this book.
    • If you are at college or university, it is likely that there are particular texts that you need to be familiar with.
    • If you are preparing for a professional qualification in a particular field, it is important to know the technical vocabulary associated with it.

3   It is essential to know how the exam works. Find out about the marking scheme, so you have a clear idea of what you need to do for each question and how much time you are going to spend on it. (And make sure the information you have about the examination is up to date.)

4   If the instructions and questions are going to be in Arabic, you will need to know what form they normally take. (You do not want to lose marks because you did not understand what you had to do.) Opposite are some key Arabic instructions often found in public examinations.

INSTRUCTIONS IN ARABIC

Read the following text.	اقرأ النَصّ التالي.
Look at the picture in front of you.	أنظُر إلى الصورة أمامك.
Listen to the announcement/news report/dialog.	استمع إلى الإعلان/الأنباء /الحوار.
Answer the following questions.	أجِب على الأسئلة التالية.
Write the appropriate word/a summary/ a commentary/an analysis.	أكتب الكلمة المناسبة/تلخيصًا/ تعليقًا/تحليلاً.
Put a ✔ in front of the correct sentence.	ضَع علامة ✔ أمام الجُمَل الصحيحة.
Fill in the blank with the appropriate word.	املأ الفراغ بالكلمة المناسبة.
Complete the following sentences.	أتمِم/أكمِل الجُمَل التالية.
Say.../ Describe...	قُل.../صِف...
Summarise.../ Define...	لَخِّص.../حَدِّد...
Write a letter/a postcard.	اكتب رسالة/بطاقة بريدية.
Explain the meaning of the following phrases/words.	اشرح معنى العبارات/الكلمات التالية.
Briefly mention the reasons.	اذكر بإيجاز الأسباب.
Answer the letter.	أجِب على الرسالة/الخطاب.
Use the following words/phrases.	استعمل الكلمات/التعبيرات التالية.
Use your own words as much as possible.	استخدَم عباراتك الشخصية على قدر الإمكان.
....as shown in the example.	...كما هو موضّح في المثال.

Answers to exercises

This section gives model answers for the exercises. Note that there are no definitive answers to the final freer exercises and compositions in each topic. Try to check your answers with an Arabic-speaking friend or teacher.

TOPIC 1 BASIC EXPRESSIONS

Exercise 1

Exercise 2

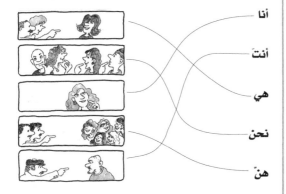

Exercise 3

١ في ٢ على ٣ بجانب ٤ تحت

Exercise 4

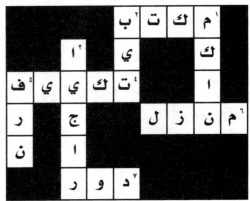

عزيزي أحمد،

عيد ميلاد سعيد !

كل عام وأنت بخير !

كيف الحال؟ أنا بخير الحمد لله .

مع تحياتي،

[your name]

TOPIC 2 HOUSE AND HOME

Exercise 1

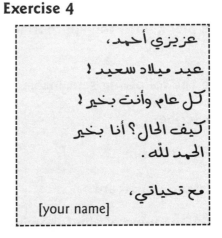

Exercise 2

Exercise 3

a البيت كبير .

b الفيلا قديم .

c المصعد مزدحم .

d الشقة جديدة ومفروشة .

e الغرفة مريحة .

Exercise 4

TOPIC 3 FAMILY AND FRIENDS

Exercise 1

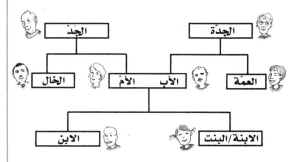

Exercise 2

Exercise 3

صديق - صاحب

صديقة - صاحبة

ولد - ابن - صبي - شابّ - مراهق

أسرة - عائلة - أقارب

Exercise 4

١ مات زَوج صَديقتي. هي أرملة .

٢ أُختي سَتَتَزوّج في سِبتَمبر. تَعَرَّفَت عَلَى خطيبها في الجامعة .

٣ أُم زوجتي هي حماتي .

٤ عندي أربعة أطفال: ثلاث بنات ووَلَد .

TOPIC 4 CHARACTER AND FEELINGS

Exercise 1

١ غضبان   ٤ ممل
٢ حزين   ٥ قبيح/غريب
٣ فرحان/مسرور   ٦ قوي

Exercise 2

١ حزين   ٤ غبي
٢ كسول   ٥ كريم
٣ هادئ

Exercise 3

(Your answers may vary.)

ايجابية جدّا	ايجابية	سلبية	سلبية جدّا
عجيب	سعيد	حزين	غضبان
مُثير	لطيف	آسِف	فظيع
مُخلص	مسرور	مؤسف	بخيل
كريم	صادق	مُمِلّ	أناني
وفي	مُضحك	ضعيف	غير مؤدّب
مجتهد	فرحان	عصبي	
مؤدّب	قوي	خجول	
شُجاع	مَشهور	غبي	
صبور	نشيط	كسول	
شريف	مَعقول	خائف	
حكيم	ظريف	ضاجّ	
	ذكي		
	هادئ		

TOPIC 5 SHOPPING

Exercise 1

١ غالٍ   ٤ مغلق   ٧ سمّاك
٢ رخيص   ٥ خيّاط   ٨ حقيبة
٣ مفتوح   ٦ زجاجة

Exercise 2

A٥   B٣   C١   D٢   E٦   F٣

Exercise 3

١ عملة   ٢ شيك   ٣ حساب   ٤ قسم

TOPIC 6 CLOTHES AND COLORS

Exercise 1

١ معطف   ٣ جوارب   ٥ حذاء   ٧ جيبة
٢ فستان   ٤ حزام   ٦ وشاح   ٨ قبّعة

Exercise 2

١ قلادة   ٢ بنطلون   ٣ مقاس   ٤ حذاء

Exercise 3

[٢] بنطلون   [١] بلوزة   [٤] قفّاز   [٥] جورب
[٣] قلادة   [٣] خاتم   [٢] تنورة   [٢] جينز
[١] سترة   [٤] حزام   [٥] حذاء   [٥] صندل
[٤] وشاح   [١] قبّعة   [١] كنزة   [٣] قرط

TOPIC 7 FOOD AND DRINK

Exercise 1

١ قهوة ٣ عصير ٥ سمك ٧ قدر

٢ شاي ٤ خبز ٦ دجاج ٨ جزر

Exercise 2

المشروبات:

عصير تفاح - حليب - ماء - كولا -عصير برتقال

الفواكه:

برتقال - عنب - تفاح - كرز - موز - فراولة

الخضروات:

بصل - فطر - قرنبيط - زيتون - جزر

Exercise 3

١ دجاج ٢ زبدة ٣ قائمة ٤ حلوى

TOPIC 8 THE BODY

Exercise 1

Exercise 2

ألمس بيدي	أذوق بلساني
أشم بأنفي	أرى بعيني
	أسمع بأذني

Exercise 3

١ رأس ٦ كتف ١١ يد

٢ عين ٧ صدر ١٢ رجل/ساق

٣ أذن ٨ ذراع ١٣ ركبة

٤ أنف ٩ بطن ١٤ قدم

٥ فم ١٠ إصبع ١٥ إصبع الرجل

TOPIC 9 HEALTH

Exercise 1

Exercise 2

(Your answers may vary.)

Things used in the treatment of illness and injury:

حبّة	علاج
دواء	مقياس الحرارة
قرص	شفاء
جراحة	

Types of injury:

جرح	كدمة
قرحة	ورم

Types of illness:

حصبة	انفلونزا
نكاف	مرض السكريّ
فيروس	سرطان
	جدري الماء

Exercise 3

١ أنا مُدمِن على التَّدخين. عادةً أدخّن أربعين سيجارة كلّ يوم.

٢ مُنذُ يَوم الحادث وهو يعاني من التوتُّر في السيَّارة.

٣ بعد العشاء شعرت فاطمة بألَم في بَطنها.

٤ ما لَكِ تعطسين و تسعلين طول الوقت؟ هل عندك برد؟

TOPIC 10 HOBBIES

Exercise 1

٤ الغوص	١ صيد السمك
٥ الموسيقى	٢ كرة السلة
٦ المطالعة	٣ المبارزة

Exercise 2

Exercise 3

(Your answers may vary.)

in a studio

الغِناء	التصوير

indoors:

لُعبة لوحية	كرة السلة
الشطرنج	مشاهدة الأفلام
	رفع الأثقال

outdoors:

الكر الطائرة	سباق الخيل
ركوب الخيل	التَّخييم

in water:

صيد السمك	التجديف
السباحة	الإبحار
	الغوص

TOPIC 11 MEDIA

Exercise 1

٥ ملف	١ لوحة مفاتيح
٦ هاتف محمول	٢ صحيفة
٧ شاشة	٣ قرص
٨ ماسحة تصوير	٤ طابعة

Exercise 2

١ أحبّ أن أشاهد التليفزيون لكنّي لا أحبّ الإعلانات!

٢ الآن كلّ الأخبار موجودة على الإنترنت.

٣ لكن جدّتي ما زالت تحبّ أن تستمع إلى الراديو.

٤ أستاذي في الجامعة يكتب مقالات لهذه المجلّة.

٥ ومن المُمكن أن تقرأ هذه المقالات في موقع المجلّة على الإنترنت أيضًا.

TOPIC 12 WEATHER AND ENVIRONMENT

Exercise 1

ب²		ة	ع	ي	ب	ط¹
ي						ق
ئ		ع⁵		ب³	ب	س⁴
ة	ب	و	ط	ر⁶		
		ا		و	ج⁷	
ظ⁸		ص	د			
ل	ص	ف⁹		ة		

Exercise 2

٣ معتدل	١ حارّ
٤ بارد	٢ دافئ

Exercise 3

١ شمس - الجو/الطقس مشمس.

٢ ثلج - الجو/الطقس مثلج.

٣ مطر - الجو/الطقس ممطر.

٤ سحابة - الجو/الطقس غائم.

TOPIC 13 LOCAL AREA

Exercise 1

٥ بنك/مصرف	١ كنيسة
٦ مطعم	٢ عمارة
٧ فندق	٣ مسجد
٨ شارع	٤ مقهى

Exercise 2

(Turn the page for answer.)

TOPIC 14 TRAVEL AND TOURISM

Exercise 1

٤ سفينة	١ طائرة
٥ سيّارة	٢ قطار
٦ دراّجة	٣ باص/أوتوبيس

Exercise 2

			ر	ف (٢)	ا (١)	س
				ح		ي
س (٤)		د	ل	ب (٣)		ا
ف			ة		ج	ح (٥)
ي						ة
ن			ف (٦)			
ة	ر	ا	ي	ز (٧)		

Exercise 3

١ السفينة في الميناء.

٢ الطائرة في المطار.

٣ القطار في المحطّة.

٤ الباص في الموقف.

TOPIC 15 EDUCATION

Exercise ١

١ كتاب   ٤ قلم

٢ مسطرة   ٥ كراسة\دفتر

٣ محّاية   ٦ قلم رصاص

Exercise ٢

١ مدرّسون/ين   ٥ أسئلة

٢ جامعات   ٦ أرقام

٣ فُصول   ٧ مَساطِر

٤ كُتُب   ٨ دَفاتِر

Exercise 3

١ أنا طالب وأدرس اَلأدب العربيّ في الجامعة.

٢ سأسافر إلى فَرَنسا لأتعلّم اللغة الفَرَنسيّة.

٣ أنا أستاذ فى كليّة الآداب وأدرّس التاريخ.

٤ أراجع للإمتِحانات في مايو.

٥ افتحي كتابك صَفحة ٦٥.

٦ أبي حفظ القُرآن في طُفولته.

٧ التلامذة يبحثون عن إجابة السؤال على الاِنتَرنَت.

٨ هل أنتَ تتعلّم اللغة الفَرَنسيّة أيضًا في المدرسة؟

TOPIC 16 WORK

Exercise ١

١ طيّار   ٥ كهربائي

٢ حلاق   ٦ محامٍ\قاضٍ

٣ بائعة زهور   ٧ ميكانيكي

٤ فنّان   ٨ حلوانية

Exercise 2

١ فنّان   ٤ مهنة

٢ بطالة   ٥ خادم

٣ حلواني   ٦ قاضٍ

Exercise 3

١ والدتي تعمل في بنك كبير في لندن.

٢ ابني محام وراتبه مُمتاز. هو يكسب أكثر مِنّي.

٣ أرباب الأعمال يدفعون الرواتب ومعاشات التقاعد.

٤ هي أكبر شركة في المدينة وتوظّف نصف السكان.

٥ يَجب أن يفصل المدير بعض العُمال بعد أن فشل المشروع.

welcome	good evening *(reply)*	how?	she
hello, hi	please	why?	they *(m, f)*
hello and welcome	thanks (for)	God willing	in
welcome to you *(reply)*	excuse me, you're welcome	happy to have met you	on
peace be on you	sorry	goodbye	from
and on you be peace *(reply)*	what? *(followed by noun)*	I	to, for
pleased to meet you	what? *(followed by verb)*	you *(m, f)*	with
good morning	who?	you *(mpl, fpl)*	above
good morning *(reply)*	where?	we	below
good evening	when?	he	beside

هِيَ	كَيفَ؟	مَساء النور	مَرحَبًا
هُم ، هُنَّ	لِماذا؟	مِن فَضلك	أهلاً
في	إن شاء اللّه	شُكرًا (على)	أهلاً وَسَهلاً
عَلى	فُرصَة سَعِيدة	عَفوًا	أهلاً بـك
مِن	مَعَ السَّلامة	آسِف	السَّلامُ عَلَيكُم
لِ	أنا	ما؟	وعَلَيكُم السَّلام
مَعَ	أنتَ ، أنتِ	ماذا؟	تَشَرَّفنا
فَوقَ	أنتُم ، أنتُنَّ	مَن؟	صَباح الخَير
تَحتَ	نَحنُ	أينَ؟	صَباح النور
بِجانِب	هُوَ	مَتى؟	مَساء الخَير

to live, reside ②	crowded ②	kitchen ②	bed ②
house ②	comfortable ②	bathroom ②	oven ②
home, dwelling ②	to consist (of) ②	garden, yard, park ②	refrigerator ②
apartment ②	floor (level) ②	street ②	table ②
villa ②	room ②	to rent ②	chair ②
apartment block ②	bedroom ②	rent (noun) ②	door ②
district, area ②	sitting room ②	furnished ②	window ②
old ②	living room ②	carpet ②	bell ②
modern ②	dining room ②	curtain ②	air-conditioning ②
quiet, calm ②	office, study, desk ②	sofa ②	elevator ②

سَرير (أسِرّة)	مَطبَخ (مَطابِخ)	مُزدحِم	سكَنَ، يَسكُن
فُرن (أفران)	حَمّام (حَمّامات)	مُريح	بَيت (بُيوت)
ثَلاجة (ثلاجات)	حديقة (حَدائق)	تَكَوّنَ، يَتَكَوّن (مِن)	منزل (مَنازِل)
مائِدة (مَوائِد)	شارِع (شَوارِع)	طابِق / دور (طَوابِق / أدوار)	شَقّة (شُقَق)
كُرسي (كَراسي)	اِستأجَرَ، يَستأجِر	غُرفة (غُرَف)	فيللا (فيللات)
باب (أبواب)	إيجار	غُرفة النّوم	عِمارة (عِمارات)
شُبّاك (شَبابيك)	مَفروش	غُرفة الجُلوس	مِنطَقة (مَناطِق)
جرَس (أجراس)	سِجادة (سِجاد)	غرفة المَعيشة/ الصالون	قَديم
تَكييف [الهواء]	سِتارة (ستائر)	السُفرة	حَديث
مِصعَد (مَصاعد)	كَنَبة (كَنَب، كَنَبات)	مكتَب (مَكاتِب)	هادِئ

family *(immediate)* ③	wife ③	grandson ③	single *(m)* ③
family *(extended)* ③	husband ③	grand-daughter ③	single *(f)* ③
relative ③	boy ③	nephew ③	child ③
father ③	girl ③	niece ③	man ③
mother ③	uncle *(paternal)* ③	bride ③	woman ③
parents ③	uncle *(maternal)* ③	bridegroom ③	youth ③
brother ③	aunt *(paternal)* ③	married ③	friend ③
sister ③	aunt *(maternal)* ③	marriage ③	to be born ③
son ③	grandfather ③	divorced ③	to die ③
daughter ③	grandmother ③	divorce ③	to get married ③

أعزَب (عُزّاب)	حَفيد (أحفاد)	زَوجة (زوجات)	أسرة (أُسَر)
عَزباء (عازِبات)	حَفيدة (حَفيدات)	زَوج (أزواج)	عائلة (عائلات)
طِفل (أطفال)	اِبن الأخ / الأخت	وَلَد (أولاد)	قَريب (أقارب)
رَجُل (رِجال)	بِنت الأخ / الأخت	بِنت (بَنات)	أب (آباء)
اِمرأة (نِساء)	عَروس (عَرائس)	عَمّ (أعمام)	أُمّ (أُمَّهات)
شابّ (شَباب، شُبّان)	عَريس (عُرسان)	خال (أخوال)	والدان /والدَين
صَديق (أصدِقاء)	مُتَزَوّج	عَمّة (عمّات)	أخ (إخوة)
وُلِدَ، يُولَد	زواج	خالة (خالات)	أُخت (أخَوات)
ماتَ، يَموت	مُطَلَّق	جَدّ (أجداد)	اِبن (أبناء)
تَزَوَّجَ، يَتَزَوّج	طلاق	جَدّة (جَدّات)	اِبنة (بَنات)

(4)	(4)	(4)	(4)
personality, character	funny	weak	afraid (of)
manners, morals	distressing	angry *(m/f)*	joyful
feelings	exciting	shy	very
not, non-, un- *(+ noun/adjective)*	amazing	generous	a little
nice	different	miserly	completely
pleased	similar	intelligent	to believe, to think
happy	strange	stupid	to think, to reflect
sad	normal, usual	lazy	to like
truthful	boring	energetic	to dislike, to hate
sorry	strong	well-behaved	to feel

خائِف (مِن)	ضَعيف	مُضحِك	شَخصيّة
	(ضُعفاء)		(شَخصيّات)
فَرحان	غَضبان / غَضبى	مُؤسِف	أخلاق
	(غِضاب)		
جِدًّا	خَجول	مُثير	شُعُور
قَليلاً	كَريم	عَجيب	غَير
	(كِرام)		
تَمامًا	بَخيل	مُختَلِف	لَطيف
	(بُخلاء)		(لُطَفاء)
اِعتَقَدَ ، يَعتَقِد	ذَكي	مُشابِه	سَعيد
	(أذكياء)		(سُعَداء)
فكّرَ ، يُفَكّر	غَبي	غَريب	مَسرور
	(أغبياء)		
أحَبَّ ، يُحِبّ	كَسول	عادي	حَزين
			(حَزانى)
كَرِهَ ، يَكرَه	نَشيط	مُمِلّ	صادِق
	(نِشاط)		
شَعَرَ ، يَشعُر بِ	مُؤدّب	قوي	آسِف
		(أقوياء)	

(5) store	(5) sale, offer	(5) wallet	(5) few, a little
(5) open	(5) seller	(5) bag, case	(5) many, much
(5) closed	(5) merchant	(5) sack, bag	(5) account, check *(total payable)*
(5) market	(5) bakery	(5) copper	(5) receipt
(5) shopping mall	(5) butcher	(5) silver	(5) reduction, discount
(5) price	(5) fishmonger	(5) gold	(5) to pay
(5) cash *(money)*	(5) grocery store	(5) leather	(5) to buy
(5) money, wealth	(5) perfume/ spice seller	(5) wood	(5) to give
(5) inexpensive	(5) tailor	(5) free	(5) to cost
(5) expensive *(indefinite/definite)*	(5) jeweller	(5) gift	(5) it is found, located *(m/f)*

قَليل	مِحفَظة (مَحافِظ)	عَرض (عُروض)	مَحَل /دُكّان (محلات/دَكاكين)
كَثير	حَقيبة (حَقائب)	بائع (باعة)	مَفتوح
حِساب (حِسابات)	كيس (أكياس)	تاجِر (تُجّار)	مَقفول /مُغلَق
إيصال (إيصالات)	نُحاس	مَخبَز (مَخابِز)	سوق (أسواق)
تَخفيض (تَخفيضات)	فِضّة	جَزّار (جَزّارون /ين)	مَركَز التَّسَوُّق (مَراكِز التَّسَوُّق)
دَفَعَ، يَدفَع	ذَهَب	سَمّاك (سمّاكون /ين)	سِعر /ثَمَن (أسعار /أثمان)
اِشترى، يَشتَري	جِلد	بَقّال (بَقّالون /ين)	نَقد (نُقود)
أعطى، يُعطي	خَشَب	عَطّار (عَطّارون /ين)	مال (أموال)
كَلَّفَ، يُكَلِّف	مَجاني	خَيّاط (خَيّاطون /ين)	رَخيص
يوجَد /توجَد	هَدِية (هَدايا)	صائغ (صُيّاغ)	غال /الغالي

clothing ⑥	jacket ⑥	headscarf ⑥ *(Islamic)*	green *(m/f)* ⑥
garments ⑥	suit ⑥	cloth/textile ⑥	brown ⑥
uniform ⑥ *(outfit)*	dress ⑥	wool ⑥	orange ⑥
underwear ⑥	skirt ⑥	cotton ⑥	violet ⑥
size, measurement ⑥	blouse ⑥	silk ⑥	pink ⑥
comfortable ⑥	coat ⑥	black *(m/f)* ⑥	purple ⑥
shirt ⑥	glove ⑥	red *(m/f)* ⑥	light *(color)* ⑥
pants ⑥	sock ⑥	yellow *(m/f)* ⑥	dark, deep *(color)* ⑥
shoe ⑥	hat ⑥	blue *(m/f)* ⑥	to wear ⑥
sandal ⑥	belt ⑥	white *(m/f)* ⑥	to take off ⑥

أخضَر / خَضراء	حِجاب (أحجبة)	سُترة / جاكيتّة (سُتَر/جاكيتّات)	ملابِس
بُنّي	قُماش (أقمشة)	بَدلة (بِدَل)	ثِياب
بُرتُقالي	صُوف	فُستان (فَساتين)	زِيّ (أزياء)
بَنَفسَجي	قُطن	تنّورة / جيبة (تنّورات/جيبات)	مَلابِس داخِليّة
وَردي	حَرير	بلوزة (بلوزات)	قِياس/مِقاس
أُرجُواني	أسوَد/سوداء	مِعطَف (مَعاطِف)	مُريح
فاتِح	أحمَر/حَمراء	قُفّاز (قُفّازات)	قَميص (قُمصان)
غامِق	أصفر/صفراء	جَورَب (جوارِب)	سِروال/بَنطَلون (بَنطَلونات/سَراويل)
لَبِسَ، يَلبَس	أزرَق/زَرقاء	قُبَّعة (قُبَّعات)	حِذاء (أحذية)
خَلَعَ، يَخلَع	أبيض/بَيضاء	حِزام (أحزمة)	صَندَل (صَنادِل)

(7) food	(7) oil	(7) fruit	(7) bananas
(7) menu, list	(7) cheese	(7) salad	(7) milk
(7) dish, course	(7) eggs	(7) onions	(7) juice
(7) meal	(7) meat	(7) potatoes	(7) water
(7) sugar	(7) lamb, mutton	(7) carrots	(7) coffee
(7) butter	(7) beef	(7) olives	(7) tea
(7) salt	(7) pork	(7) grapes	(7) alcohol
(7) pepper	(7) chicken	(7) apples	(7) dessert, sweet
(7) bread	(7) fish	(7) oranges	(7) to eat
(7) rice	(7) vegetables	(7) lemons	(7) to drink

طَعام/أكل	زَيت	فَواكِه	مَوز
قائِمة (قَوائِم)	جُبنة	سَلَطة	حَليب
طَبَق (أطباق)	بَيض	بَصَل	عَصير
وَجبة (وَجبات)	لَحم	بَطّاطا/ بَطاطِس	ماء
سُكَّر	(لحم) ضَأني	جَزَر	قَهوة
زُبدة	(لحم) بَقَريّ	زَيتُون	شاي
مِلح	لحم الخِنزير	عِنَب	كُحُول
فِلفِل	دَجاج	تُفّاح	حَلوى
خُبز	سَمَك	بُرتُقال	أكَلَ، يأكُل
أرُزّ	خُضرَوات	لَيمون	شَرِبَ، يشرَب

body ⑧	belly, stomach ⑧	finger ⑧	lip ⑧
skeleton ⑧	arm *(f)* ⑧	toe ⑧	bone ⑧
head ⑧	leg *(f)* ⑧	thumb ⑧	skin ⑧
face ⑧	foot *(f)* ⑧	chest ⑧	to see ⑧
eye *(f)* ⑧	knee ⑧	back ⑧	to hear ⑧
ear *(f)* ⑧	hand *(f)* ⑧	heart ⑧	to smell ⑧
nose ⑧	elbow ⑧	hair ⑧	to taste ⑧
mouth ⑧	wrist ⑧	brain ⑧	to move *(something)* ⑧
tongue ⑧	shoulder ⑧	blood ⑧	to move *(yourself)* ⑧
neck ⑧	tooth ⑧	lung ⑧	to touch ⑧

شَفة (شِفاه)	إصبَع (أصابِع)	بَطن (بُطون)	جِسم (أجسام)
عَظم (عِظام)	إصبَع الرّجل (أصابِع الرِجل)	ذِراع (أذرُع)	هَيكل عَظميّ (هَياكِل عَظميّة)
جِلد (جُلود)	إبهام	رِجل / ساق (أرجُل / سيقان)	رَأس (رُؤُوس)
رأى ، يرى	صَدر (صُدُور)	قَدَم (أقدام)	وَجه (وُجوه)
سَمِعَ ، يَسمَع	ظَهر (ظُهُور)	رُكبة (رُكَب)	عَين (عُيُون)
شَمَّ ، يَشُمّ	قَلب (قُلوب)	يَد (أيادٍ)	أُذُن (آذان)
ذاقَ ، يَذُوق	شَعر	كوع / مِرفَق (أكواع / مَرافِق)	أَنف (أُنوف)
حَرَّكَ ، يُحَرِّك	مُخّ	رُسغ (أرساغ)	فَم (أفواه)
تَحَرَّك ، يَتَحَرَّك	دَم	كِتف (أكتاف)	لِسان (ألسنة)
لَمَسَ ، يَلمَس	رِئة (رِئات)	سِنّ (أسنان)	رَقَبة (رِقاب)

(9) health	(9) pulse	(9) accident	(9) addicted (to)
(9) healthy	(9) headache	(9) hospital	(9) smoking
(9) illness	(9) injury	(9) doctor	(9) diet
(9) sick, patient (noun)	(9) wound	(9) nurse	(9) to suffer (from)
(9) cold	(9) pain	(9) ambulance	(9) to take (medicine, etc.)
(9) congested (nose)	(9) painful	(9) operation, surgery	(9) to fall
(9) afflicted with	(9) medicine	(9) doctor's office	(9) to break
(9) fever	(9) pill	(9) cure	(9) to cough
(9) diarrhoea	(9) tablet	(9) treatment	(9) to swallow
(9) cough	(9) thermometer	(9) habit	(9) to smoke

مُدمِن (على)	حادث (حَوادث)	نَبض	صِحّة
تَدخين	مُستشفى (مُتَسَشفيات)	صُداع	بِصِحّة جَيّدة
رجيم	طَبيب (أطبّاء)	إصابة (إصابات)	مَرض (أمراض)
عانَى، يُعاني (مِن)	مُمرِّضة (مُمرِّضات)	جُرح (جِراح)	مَريض (مَرْضى)
تناول، يَتَناوَل	سَيّارة إسعاف	ألَم (آلام)	بَرد
وَقَعَ، يَقَع	جِراحة (جِراحات)	مُؤلِم	مَزكوم
كَسَر، يَكسِر	عِيادة (عِيادات)	دَواء (أدوِية)	مُصاب بِ
سَعَلَ، يَسعُل	شِفاء (أشفِية)	حَبّة (حُبوب)	حُمّى
بَلَعَ، يَبلَع	عِلاج (عِلاجات)	قُرص (أقراص)	إسهال
دَخّنَ، يُدَخّن	عادة (عادات)	مِقياس الحَرارة	سُعال

hobby (10)	volleyball (10)	musical instrument (10)	drawing (10)
spare time (10)	running, jogging (10)	flute (10)	photography (10)
sport (10)	skiing (10)	violin (10)	hunting (10)
sporty, sportsman (10)	swimming (10)	guitar (10)	fishing (10)
game (10)	dancing (10)	piano (10)	chess (10)
player (10)	music (10)	horn, trumpet (10)	backgammon (10)
team (10)	singing (10)	drum (10)	board game (10)
training, practice (10)	group, band (10)	reading (10)	to play (a sport) (10)
soccer (10)	song (10)	watching movies (10)	to play (an instrument) (10)
basketball (10)	singer (10)	play (theater) (10)	to be interested in (10)

رَسم	آلة موسيقية	الكُرة الطائرة	هِواية
	(آلات موسيقية)		(هِوايات)
تَصوير	فلوت	جري/عَدو	وَقت الفَراغ
صَيد	كمان	تَزلُّج	رِياضة
صَيد السَمَك	جيتار	سِباحة	رِياضيّ
شَطرَنج	بِيانو	رَقص	لُعبة
			(ألعاب)
طاوِلة (الزهر)	بوق	مُوسيقى	لاعِب
	(أبواق)		(لاعِبون/ين)
لُعبة لوحية	طَبلة	غِناء	فَريق
	(طُبول)		(فِرَق)
لَعِبَ ، يَلعَب	قِراءة/مُطالَعَة	فِرقة	تدريب
		(فِرَق)	(تَدريبات)
عَزَفَ ، يَعزِف على	مُشاهَدة الأفلام	أُغنِية	كُرة القَدَم
		(أغانٍ)	
اِهتَمّ ، يَهتَمّ بـ	مَسرَحيّة	مُغَنٍّ	كُرة السَلّة
	(مَسرَحيّات)	(مُغَنّيون/ين)	

media	press	internet	director
communication	news item *(pl. = news)*	website	producer
technology	newspaper	channel	correspondent
broadcast, broadcasting	magazine	telephone	photographer
television	article	cellphone	broadcaster, announcer
radio	computer	advertisement, announcement	to watch
sound	keyboard	program, show	to listen
tape	screen	direct *(broadcast, etc.)*	to record
disc	printer	journalist	to print
recorder	file	editor	to publish

مُخرِج	إنترنت	صِحافة	وَسائِل الإعلام
(مُخرِجون/ين)			
مُنتِج	مَوقِع	خَبَر	اِتِّصال
(مُنتِجون/ين)	(مَواقِع)	(أخبار)	(اِتِّصالات)
مُراسِل	قَناة	جَريدة/صَحيفة	تكنولوجيا
(مُراسِلون/ين)	(قَنَوات)	(جَرائِد/ صُحُف)	
مُصَوِّر	هاتِف/تِلِفون	مَجَلّة	إذاعة
(مُصَوِّرون/ين)	(هَواتِف/ تلفونات)	(مَجَلات)	(إذاعات)
مُذيع	جَوّال/مَحمول	مَقالة	تليفِزيون
(مُذيعون/ين)		(مَقالات)	(تليفِزيونات)
شاهَدَ ، يُشاهِد	إعلان	كُمبيوتِر/ حاسوب	راديو
	(إعلانات)		
اِستَمَعَ ، يَستَمِع	بَرنامَج	لَوحة مَفاتيح	صَوت
	(بَرامِج)		(أصوات)
سَجَّلَ ، يُسَجِّل	مُباشِر	شاشة	شَريط
		(شاشات)	(أشرِطة)
طَبَعَ ، يَطبَع	صُحُفي/صِحافي	طابِعة	قُرص
	(صُحُفيون/ين)	(طَوابِع)	(أقراص)
نَشَرَ ، يَنشُر	مُحَرِّر	مِلَفّ	مُسَجِّل
	(مُحَرِّرون/ين)	(مِلَفّات)	(مُسَجِّلات)

weather ⑫	heat ⑫	rain ⑫	water ⑫
environment ⑫	hot ⑫	ice, snow ⑫	air ⑫
nature ⑫	clear, fine ⑫	sunny ⑫	earth, dust ⑫
atmosphere, weather ⑫	temperature ⑫	cloudy ⑫	fire ⑫
climate ⑫	cold (noun) ⑫	rainy ⑫	wind ⑫
season ⑫	cold (adjective) ⑫	icy, snowy ⑫	storm ⑫
spring ⑫	warm ⑫	sky ⑫	pollution ⑫
summer ⑫	moderate, temperate ⑫	earth, land ⑫	cause, reason ⑫
autumn, fall ⑫	humidity ⑫	sun ⑫	to cause ⑫
winter ⑫	cloud ⑫	moon ⑫	to protect ⑫

ماء (مِياه)	مَطر	حَرارة	طَقس
هَواء	ثَلج	حارّ / ساخِن	بيئة
تُراب (أتربة)	مُشمِس	صَحو	طَبيعة
نار (نِيران)	غائِم	دَرَجة الحَرارة	جَو (أجواء)
رِيح (رِياح)	مُمطِر	بَرد / بُرودة	مُناخ (مُناخات)
عاصِفة (عَواصِف)	مُثلِج	بارِد	فَصل (فُصول)
تَلَوُّث	سَماء (سماوات)	دافِئ	الرَبيع
سَبَب (أسباب)	أرض (أراضٍ)	مُعتَدِل	الصَيف
سَبَّبَ، يُسَبِّب	شَمس	رُطوبة	الخَريف
حَمى، يَحمي	قَمَر (أقمار)	سَحابة (سُحُب)	الشِتاء

region (13)	town hall (13)	mosque (13)	palace (13)
place (13)	school (13)	church (13)	farm (13)
city (13)	hotel (13)	club (13)	mountain (13)
countryside (13)	restaurant (13)	park, garden (13)	river (13)
village (13)	café, coffee shop (13)	library, bookstore (13)	north (13)
street (13)	pharmacy (13)	downtown (13)	west (13)
road, way (13)	bank (13)	post office (13)	south (13)
traffic (13)	police station (13)	movie theater (13)	east (13)
block (offices, apartments, etc.) (13)	gas station (13)	theater (13)	to roam around (13)
building (13)	beach (13)	bridge (13)	to get lost (13)

قَصر (قُصور)	مَسجِد /جامِع (مَساجِد/جوامِع)	مَبنى البَلَديّة	مِنطَقة (مَناطِق)
مَزرَعة (مَزارِع)	كَنيسة (كَنائِس)	مَدرسة (مَدارِس)	مكان (أماكِن)
جَبَل (جِبال)	نادٍ (نوادٍ)	فُندُق (فَنادِق)	مَدينة (مُدُن)
نَهر (أنهار)	حَديقة (حَدائِق)	مَطعَم (مَطاعِم)	ريف (أرياف)
شَمال	مكتَبة (مكتَبات)	مقهى (مَقاهٍ)	قَرية (قُرًى)
غَرب	وَسَط المدينة	صَيدَليّة (صَيدَليّات)	شارِع (شَوارِع)
جَنوب	مكتَب البَريد (مَكاتِب البَريد)	بَنك / مَصرَف (بُنُوك/مَصارِف)	طَريق (طُرُق)
شَرق	سينما	مَركَز شُرطة (مَراكِز شُرطة)	مُرور
تَجَوَّلَ ، يَتَجَوَّل	مَسرَح (مَسارِح)	مَحطّة بَنزين (مَحطّات بَنزين)	عِمارة (عمارات)
تاهَ، يَتوه	جِسر (جُسور)	شاطِئ (شَواطِئ)	مَبنى (مَبانٍ)

travel (14)	plane (14)	ticket (14)	straight on (14)
tourism (14)	boat (14)	one-way (14)	before (14)
journey, trip (14)	ship (14)	roundtrip (14)	after (14)
visit (14)	bus (14)	sea (14)	to go (14)
country (14)	airport (14)	seaside, shore (14)	to walk (14)
traveler (14)	stop (bus, train, etc.) (14)	baggage (14)	to return (14)
car (14)	station (14)	camera (14)	to travel (14)
taxi (14)	port, harbor (14)	postcard (14)	to ride, to catch, to board (14)
bicycle (14)	passport (14)	fast (14)	to spend (time) (14)
train (14)	visa (14)	slow (14)	to arrive (14)

عَلى طول	تَذكِرة (تَذاكِر)	طائِرة (طائِرات)	سَفَر
قَبلَ	ذَهاب	قارِب (قَوارِب)	سِياحة
بَعدَ	ذَهاب وإياب / وعَودة	سَفينة (سُفُن)	رِحلة (رِحلات)
ذَهَبَ ، يَذهَب	بَحر (بِحار)	باص/أوتوبيس (باصات/أوتوبيسات)	زِيارة (زِيارات)
مَشى ، يَمشي	شاطِئ (شَواطِئ)	مَطار (مطارات)	بَلَد (بِلاد/بُلدان)
رَجَع ، يَرجَع / عاد ، يعود	أمتِعَة	مَوقِف (مواقِف)	مُسافِر (مُسافِرون/ين)
سافَرَ ، يُسافِر	آلة تَصوير / كامِيرا	مَحَطّة (مَحَطّات)	سَيّارة (سَيّارات)
رَكِبَ، يركَب	بِطاقة بَريديّة	ميناء (موانٍ)	تاكسي / سَيّارة أُجرة
قَضى ، يَقضي	سَريع	جَواز السَّفَر (جوازات السَّفَر)	دَرّاجة (درّاجات)
وَصَلَ ، يَصِل	بَطيء	تأشيرة (تأشيرات)	قِطار (قِطارات)

(15) student *(college)*	(15) semester, class	(15) notebook	(15) Arabic language
(15) student *(school)*	(15) lesson	(15) dictionary	(15) history
(15) teacher	(15) homework	(15) letter *(of the alphabet)*	(15) geography
(15) professor, teacher	(15) book	(15) number	(15) science
(15) primary school	(15) exercise book	(15) question	(15) biology
(15) junior high school	(15) pen	(15) answer	(15) chemistry
(15) high school	(15) pencil	(15) exam	(15) physics
(15) college, faculty	(15) eraser	(15) mathematics	(15) to study
(15) university	(15) pencil sharpener	(15) literature	(15) to teach
(15) class, classroom	(15) ruler	(15) English language	(15) to learn

اللُغة العَرَبيّة	دَفتَر (دَفاتِر)	فَصل (فُصول)	طالِب (طُلّاب، طَلَبة)
تاريخ	قاموس (قَواميس)	درَس (دُروس)	تِلميذ (تَلاميذ)
جُغرافيا	حَرف (حُروف)	واجِب مَدرَسيّ	مُعَلِّم / مُدرِّس (مُعَلِّمون/ين)
عُلوم	رَقَم (أرقام)	كِتاب (كُتُب)	أُستاذ (أساتِذة)
عِلم الأحياء	سُؤال (أسئِلة)	كُرّاسة (كُرّاسات)	مَدرَسة ابتِدائيّة
عِلم الكيمياء	إجابة (إجابات)	قَلَم (أقلام)	مَدرَسة إعداديّة
عِلم الفيزياء	امتِحان (امتِحانات)	قَلَم رَصاص	مَدرَسة ثانويّة
دَرَسَ، يَدرُس	رياضيّات	مَحاية (مَحّايات)	كُلِّية (كُلِّيات)
دَرَّسَ، يُدَرِّس / عَلَّمَ، يُعَلِّم	أدَب (آداب)	بَرّاية (بَرّايات)	جامِعة (جامِعات)
تَعَلَّمَ، يَتَعَلَّم	اللُغة الإنجليزيّة	مِسطَرة (مَساطِر)	صَفّ (صُفوف)

(16) work	(16) secretary	(16) engineer	(16) farmer
(16) profession	(16) employee	(16) pilot	(16) artist
(16) job, position	(16) expert	(16) driver	(16) unemployment
(16) company	(16) specialist	(16) mechanic	(16) unemployed
(16) branch	(16) businessman	(16) electrician	(16) retirement
(16) office	(16) business-woman	(16) plumber	(16) retired
(16) experience	(16) researcher	(16) cook	(16) salary
(16) trade	(16) trader	(16) confectioner	(16) (working) hours
(16) manager, director	(16) lawyer	(16) barber	(16) to work
(16) worker	(16) judge	(16) florist	(16) to employ

مُزارِع (مُزارِعون/ين)	مُهَندِس (مُهَندِسون/ين)	سِكرِتَيرة (سِكرِتَيرات)	عَمَل /شُغل (أعمال / أشغال)
فَنّان (فَنّانون/ين)	طَيّار (طَيّارون/ين)	مُوَظَّف (مُوَظَّفون/ين)	مِهنة (مِهَن)
بَطالة	سائِق (سائِقون/ين)	خَبير (خُبَراء)	وَظيفة (وَظائف)
عاطِل	ميكانيكي (ميكانيكيون/ين)	مُتخَصِّص (مُتخصِّصون/ين)	شَرِكة (شَرِكات)
تَقاعُد	كَهرَبائي (كَهرَبائيون/ين)	رَجُل أعمال (رِجال أعمال)	فَرع (فُروع)
مُتقاعِد	سَبّاك (سَبّاكون/ين)	سَيِّدة أعمال (سَيِّدات أعمال)	مكتَب (مكاتب)
راتِب (رواتِب)	طَبّاخ (طَبّاخون/ين)	باحِث (باحِثون/ين)	خِبرة
دوام	حَلَواني (حَلَوانيون/ين)	تاجِر (تُجّار)	تِجارة
عَمِلَ، يَعمَل	حَلاق (حَلاقون/ين)	مُحام (مُحامون/ين)	مُدير (مُدَراء)
وَظَّفَ، يُوَظِّف	بائع زُهُور (باعة زُهُور)	قاضٍ (قُضاة)	عامِل (عُمّال)